Gone Missing in New York

Marianna Boncek

Schiffer ®
Publishing Ltd

4880 Lower Valley Road, Atglen, Pennsylvania 19310

Dedication

~ To Liz and Rachel... my two luminaries
~ To Freddie Holmes... I will never stop looking
~ To Todd Matthews... the guardian angel of the missing and their families.

Schiffer Books are available at special discounts for bulk purchases for sales promotions or premiums. Special editions, including personalized covers, corporate imprints, and excerpts can be created in large quantities for special needs. For more information contact the publisher:

Published by Schiffer Publishing Ltd.
4880 Lower Valley Road
Atglen, PA 19310
Phone: (610) 593-1777; Fax: (610) 593-2002
E-mail: Info@schifferbooks.com

For the largest selection of fine reference books on this and related subjects,
please visit our website at:
www.schifferbooks.com
We are always looking for people to write books on new and related subjects.
If you have an idea for a book,
please contact us at **proposals@schifferbooks.com**

This book may be purchased from the publisher.
Include $5.00 for shipping.
Please try your bookstore first.
You may write for a free catalog.

In Europe, Schiffer books are distributed by
Bushwood Books
6 Marksbury Ave.
Kew Gardens
Surrey TW9 4JF England
Phone: 44 (0) 20 8392 8585; Fax: 44 (0) 20 8392 9876
E-mail: info@bushwoodbooks.co.uk
Website: www.bushwoodbooks.co.uk

Other Schiffer Books by the Author:
Spooky Hudson Valley, 978-0-7643-3384-2, $14.99

Other Schiffer Books on Related Subjects:
Briar Patch: The Murder that Would Not Die, 978-0-7643-3782-6, $24.99

Copyright © 2011 by Marianna Boncek
Library of Congress Control Number: 2011933098

Designed by Mark David Bowyer
Type set in American Typewriter Medium / New Baskerville BT

ISBN: 978-0-7643-3837-3
Printed in the United States of America

Contents

Part One

Gone Missing

This book started as a quest to understand a childhood mystery. In 1955, six years before I was born, not far from my childhood home in a very rural corner of the Sullivan County Catskills, Freddie Holmes, just 22-months-old, disappeared without a trace. By the time I was old enough to hear his story, Freddie's disappearance had become a legend. To scare us into staying close to home, my father would drive my brothers and me by the house, unoccupied by this time, and retell the story of the missing boy. While it frightened us at the moment, it did little to stop us from wandering around the neighborhood.

As soon as I was old enough, I started my own search for Freddie. Like most children, I never connected the fact that if a "little boy" could go missing, I could, too. I felt some sort of childish moral obligation to look for Freddie. Being only a child at the time, I had no idea the complexities involved in searching for missing people. Nor could I begin to comprehend the myriad of reasons a two-year-old might go missing in the first place. I did a lot of childish searching, looking for the lost boy. I always dreamed of finding him; a bone under a bush or in a pile of old leaves. Even as a child, I understood the possibilities of finding him alive were slim to none.

The house Freddie "Tookie" Holmes disappeared from on Denman Mountain Road, Grahamsville, on May 25, 1955.

My child's mind told me that people just do not disappear. Of course, as I grew older, I learned people disappear everyday and some leave behind no clues as to what happened to them. Of course, when Freddie went missing, there wasn't the forensic science, laws, and resources available to aid in the search and rescue of a missing child. Though it has been a long time since I started looking for Freddie, I still believe that people do not just disappear… I still believe that there are clues and witnesses that can help us solve these most frustrating and puzzling of mysteries.

Forty years later, when I returned to my search for Freddie, I believed that his disappearance would be a rare and singular occurrence. I believed I would be writing a single article about an unusual circumstance. I could not have been more wrong. The more I looked into the plight of the missing, the more I realized this country is facing a silent epidemic. Everywhere, everyday, people disappear. The more I researched the plight of the missing, the more overwhelmed I became. Believing that it was only logical that all missing Americans were monitored by a single police or governmental agency, I started to search for that agency. What I found was shocking — there is *no* centralized police agency or governmental organization to help search for the missing, raise public awareness, or raise funds to assist in the search of the missing and relief for their families. Searching for the missing is "hit or miss." While there are many excellent agencies, both public and private, none of them are centralized, and if centralized, they are far from comprehensive. There is no policy (or law) that requires all law enforcement agencies to share information to assist in the search for missing. For example, a family in New York may never know that their loved one is in an unmarked grave in California because law enforcement agencies are not required to exchange information. Thus, this book changed from a quest to tell the story of one missing boy into the desire to help the missing everywhere. This book is to help raise awareness of the plight of the missing. It is also a resource book for those interested in helping or for families and friends of the missing. By raising awareness and getting involved, we can all help end this silent epidemic.

This book deals only with disappearances throughout the state of New York. My hope is by sharing these stories someone will come forward with information, no matter how small, to help these families find their loved ones. While familial and parental abductions and run-aways are no less serious and traumatizing, those stories are out of the scope of this book. However, the search advice, organizations, and techniques listed here will help all the families of the missing — no matter what the circumstances is of their disappearance.

Who Are the Missing?

Missing New Yorkers are all ages from infants to the very old. They are male and female, Black, White, Hispanics, and Asian. They are rich, poor, and middle class. They are city folks, farmers, and suburbanites. There is no county in New York that does not have at least one missing person. They have gone missing in morning hours, during the afternoon, and late at night. They have disappeared on the way to the store, to work, to school, and on their way home. They all have one in thing in common — they need to be found so that their loved ones' minds can be put to rest.

There is no typical missing person or typical circumstances under which a person goes missing. People go missing for many reasons and under a myriad of circumstances and, as odd as it sounds, some people choose to disappear. A person may be a child run-away or an adult who decides to leave his or her life and cut off contact with family and friends. Other people are victims of crimes, abductions, and murders. People with Alzheimer's disease or dementia can become disoriented and wander off. Though rare, people do develop amnesia from an accident or illness and can't remember who they are. People die accidentally, without any identification, and investigators are left without any clues to their identity. There seems to be as many ways to disappear as there are people who are missing. Each missing person has gone missing under a unique set of circumstances. However, all missing people leave behind family and friends whose lives are irrevocably changed. When a person goes missing, the lives of their loved ones come to a crashing halt; many families spend all their emotional strength and financial resources searching for that loved one. The suffering the family members endure is some of the worst emotional suffering I have ever witnessed. People age prematurely while some develop illnesses and even die due to stress-related problems. Many times families are torn apart as they try to manage the search for their loved one and continue on with their own lives. Suspicion is often, wrongly or rightly, thrown upon a family member. In desperation, many families are taken advantage of by scammers pretending to be psychics or private investigators. Most of these families suffer in unbearable silence.

The missing placard the Turks keep in their front yard of their daughter, Audrey Herron, missing since August 29, 2002 from Catskill.

issing Persons Report

A Staggering Epidemic

The plight of the missing is a national — and *silent* — epidemic. According to the Federal Bureau of Investigations National Crime Information Center, as of January 1, 2009 there were 102,864 active missing persons cases. However, these only represent the cases reported to the FBI. Local and state police agencies are not required to make reports to the FBI. Some experts have suggested that the actual number of missing Americans could number near one million. There is no area in the United States that this epidemic has not reached. Everywhere, someone is missing. Everywhere, a family struggles to understand and bring their loved one home.

While New York State keeps comprehensive statistics on missing children, it does not do the same for its missing adults. In 2008 alone, 20,414 children went missing. While the vast majority of those were runaways, among those statistics were: one stranger abduction, 285 lost children, and 1,102 children missing under unknown circumstances. That is 1,388 children missing under mysterious or dangerous circumstances *for a single year.* That averages to just over three children a day from New York State *alone*. If these figures were attached to a disease, there would be a public outcry for our government to step in and find a cure.

At the time of this publication, the New York State Police website lists fifty-two missing persons, but this is far from being comprehensive. The New York City Police website, which is separate from the State Police, lists twenty-three recent cases of missing persons. The Missing and Exploited Children's website lists fifty-two children missing from New York under dangerous and/or mysterious circumstances, but this figure does not include children who have been abducted by non-custodial relatives. The Charley Project, a privately maintained online database, lists 341 missing New Yorkers. However, wherever you look, these numbers are woefully inadequate. No organization, website, or agency consistently lists every single person missing under mysterious or dangerous circumstances. There is no single, centralized place where family, the public, or authorities can go to find information about each and every missing New Yorker. Missing people "slip through the cracks" each day, leaving their family members frustrated, bitter, and angry as they look for answers. The number of missing New Yorkers is easily estimated in the thousands. This epidemic is out of control. We owe every missing American a name, a comprehensive search, and, if at all possible, a homecoming.

What Happens When Someone Goes Missing?

Before modern technology and communications, it was very easy to become a missing person. People migrated from country to country and lost track of family and friends. People became victims of disaster or crime and were buried unidentified. When a person went missing, the best the family could do is organize their own search. If the person went missing locally, family and friends would gather and formulate their own search parties. Often times, if the family did not have the means, the search was only cursory. Even when the missing person was reported to authorities, there was nothing much the police could do, but with the birth of police investigative techniques, forensic science, and advanced technology, searching for the missing has changed drastically. With the use of modern technology, many more people than ever before are being located and many unidentified remains are being identified and returned to their loved ones for a proper burial.

Unless a person is abducted and the abduction is witnessed or a child becomes lost, it often takes awhile to realize a person is missing. Sometimes it is a short period of time: a child did not come home from school or a person did not show up for work. Other times, it can be days or even weeks before someone realizes that he or she has not seen or heard from a person. The most important thing a person can do is to notify the authorities as soon as he or she realizes a person is missing. A missing person may be in danger and the sooner the search begins the better the chances are of locating that person safe and sound.

The police will come and speak with the person who filed the report. The first place the police start their search is the last known location of the missing person. However, in most cases, the police will ask to search the home of the missing person, as well as the last place the person was seen. It is extremely uncomfortable to the family of the missing to have the police searching through their personal space. Many times, the family feels like they are being accused. However, in a surprising number of cases, the missing person or a clue to his/her whereabouts is found in

issing Persons Report

the home. Police are trained investigators. They are not just "looking blindly" — they are looking for hints and clues that will help them find the missing person…things the family might have overlooked might be important to the investigation and search.

The police will start by asking about the basics, such as: When was the last time the missing person was seen or heard from? And by whom? Police will also ask why the person is believed to be missing, not just have gone somewhere on his or her own. The investigators will ask for a recent picture of the person, phone numbers, etc. and families should do their best to provide this information. There may only be one or two officers at the home during the initial stages of the search; however, if a full-scale search is initiated this can quickly grow to several dozen.

Family members and close friends of the missing will be asked seemingly endless questions. The police must rule out all scenarios, and there are dishonest people in the world and the police deal with these people everyday. Ruling out people is very important. Once a person is ruled out as being involved, the police can focus their time and energy elsewhere. Also, many people do just "take a break" from life and go off on their own for awhile. Police do not want to waste precious time and resources on a person who is not truly missing. Every search is different because every missing person is different. Occasionally, people are asked to take lie detector tests.

As the search progresses, it will increase in complexity. It may start out with just a few police and firefighters. The police may even decide to use volunteers, particularly if the search area is very large. Other decisions are made, based on information the police receive. Sometimes a very wide search is undertaken using police, firefighters, forest rangers, and other professional and volunteer organizations. Search dogs may be used if authorities feel they will be helpful. Police may search many different areas over several days, weeks, or months. Sometimes difficult weather can hamper searches. Here in New York, once the snow falls, it is difficult to conduct comprehensive searches. It is also difficult to conduct searches in the summer due to dense foliage in wooded areas. Once initial comprehensive searches are made following the disappearance, if a person is not located quickly, police may wait until the spring, when the snow has melted and the vegetation has not begun to grow, or in the autumn, after the first frost but before the first snow falls. It is important to understand that the police are not just looking for a body. They are also looking for clues, clothing, a wallet — anything that belonged to the missing person that will tell them where the missing person may have gone.

If the missing person is not found quickly, a decision will be made about the media. If the police determine that a child has been abducted,

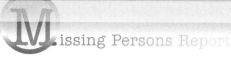

they will issue an Amber Alert. An Amber Alert (named after nine-year-old Amber Hagerman, who was abducted and murdered in Texas) is a coordinated effort by public and private organizations to get the information out about an abducted child and the circumstances of his/her abduction to as many outlets as possible. Broadcast notices are sent to radio and television stations, the emergency alert system, electronic traffic signs, billboards, toll booth workers — they can even be sent via text messages. Amber Alerts are quick and effective. However, an Amber Alert is only activated when authorities are sure the child has been abducted. If the missing person is an adult, the police agency and family usually make the decision on how the media will be involved. The more endangered the police feel a missing adult is, the more likely they are to involve the media.

Only one police agency will become the lead investigative agency. This agency will assign detectives to the case, plan the investigation, and follow up on leads. Some agencies have limited resources, such as town police, while others, like the State Police, have a wider variety of sources to aid in the search. Smaller agencies may call on larger ones to assist in the search and investigation.

I'd like to say that all missing person reports are acted upon quickly and efficiently and all police organizations are fully trained to conduct a full-scale search. While most police agencies are competent, organized, and professional, not every missing person's case has been treated professionally and thoroughly as it should have been. In the unbelievable case of Judith Guerin, the police wouldn't even take a missing person's report until thirteen years after she had been missing This is just one example of an agency letting a missing person slip desperately through the cracks of justice. This is why we must advocate for a single governmental agency that tracks all missing New Yorkers and trains all police agencies in every corner of the state in proper procedures in looking for the missing.

Part Two

The Missing

"There is no time limit to solving a mystery"
~ the motto of the Doe Network

This part of the book highlights cases of actual missing people. It's easy to talk about the missing as numbers. While the numbers themselves are terrifying, this is my attempt to put a human face on missing individuals. People often asked me for my criteria for selecting missing people for this book. I would have liked to include all missing New Yorkers, because they all deserve their story to be told. They all deserve a homecoming. I chose cases that fit two very simple criteria; that the person be a New Yorker missing under mysterious and that the family was willing to share their stories with the public. I encourage you, after reading these stories to visit The Charley Project website and the Doe Network website (full information listed in the Sourcebook section of this book) and read about all missing people everywhere. By learning about these people, their lives and the loved ones they left behind, I hope you will become active in helping bring them home.

MISSING

This is the house on Hunter Street where Barbara Hartman Brown went missing from sometime in the 1860s.

HAVE YOU SEEN THIS WOMAN?

Barbara Hartmann Brown

Race: White

Sex: Female

Last Seen: Hunter Street, Rondout (Kingston), New York

Circumstances of Disappearance: Barbara's husband arrived home to find the house in order and Barbara missing. Nothing out of the ordinary has ever been found. If you know anything about Barbara Hartman Brown, please contact Barbara's great-great-great granddaughter, Elizabeth Sanborn, at forgottendreamr@yahoo.com or her great-great grandson, Vincent A. Sanborn, at 579 South Hill Road, Grahamsville, New York 12740, (845)985-0563 or the author at marianna.boncek@gmail.com.

Barbara Hartmann Brown

Note from the author: Unlike the rest of the stories featured here, this story is told in first-person, as Barbara is a member of my extended family. Also, today the family spells "Hartmann" with one 'n', for Hartman.

Sometime between the years 1863 and 1870 my daughters' great-great-great grandmother (on their father's side), Barbara Hartmann Brown, disappeared. While many of the details are now lost forever, almost a century and a half has passed, the hollowness this unsolved mystery created still lingers. The pain of a missing family member is passed on from generation to generation. While the intense pain of the loss lessens, the feeling that something is deeply missing, that the family is not complete, lingers.

John A. Brown, whose name was Americanized from the German Johann Braun, had spent a great deal of time becoming a successful blacksmith. Like many German immigrants, he found his way to the Rondout district of Kingston, New York. In the mid-1800s, the Rondout district was a distinct and separate village from the city of Kingston. It is located along the shores of the Rondout Creek, which empties into the Hudson River. This is also where the Delaware and Hudson Canal came to an end. Because of its location, it was a prime spot to locate businesses that relied on the Hudson River for transport to New York City and beyond. The small town was just becoming a "boomtown" when John arrived. Local bluestone, cement, and brick were shipped from Island Dock, a man-made dock in the middle of the Rondout Creek. Coal from central Pennsylvania made its way to the Hudson via canal and was loaded onto boats. Warehouses were constructed to store products ready to be shipped. Other businesses, such as ship-building and meat packing, sprung up seemingly overnight.

John was a skilled blacksmith and his services were quickly in demand.

He set up shop on Abeel Street. John was a serious man. He worked six days a week, attended church on Sunday, and sent money home with his letters to his family still in Germany. By age thirty-seven, he ran a thriving blacksmith shop, had saved a tidy sum, and owned several pieces of property, some of which he rented out for added income. He had long been ready to settle down, but he had been unable to find a serious German girl who had the same drive and goals that he did. He wrote to his family in Germany about his desire and they wrote back about a young German girl, Barbara Hartmann, who was looking to come to America.

Barbara Hartmann had been an infant when John had left Germany as a young man. Her family was eager to immigrate to America after hearing stories of the success of other Germans. In order to come to America, an immigrant needed to have a sponsor and a job or, as in Barbara's case, a waiting fiancé. Once here, Barbara would be able to open the door to America for her family by becoming their sponsor and finding them jobs. Headed out towards what was to be a prosperous future, Barbara mounted a ship alone to become a bride to a man she had never seen and was seventeen years her senior.

Upon arriving, John and Barbara were married in St. Mary's Catholic Church. By all accounts, the marriage was a happy one. About a year after their marriage, their first child, Eliza, arrived. After Eliza, children started to arrive on a regular basis every few years until the family grew to six children. Family members recall John as a generous man. He helped out newcomers to the country, gave generously to the local church, and made sure his wife and children lived comfortably. He worked hard, what we would call a "workaholic" in today's society. However, many immigrants worked long hours, usually six days a week; it was not uncommon in the neighborhood. The Browns were well regarded by their neighbors and friends.

One evening, after a long day's work, John arrived home to find the house immaculately cleaned, the children bathed and fed, and the baby, just six months old, sitting happily in the highchair. However, his wife was nowhere to be found. He questioned the children repeatedly, but they were only able to report that their mother had "gone out." It was highly unusual for Barbara to leave her children home alone, particularly the baby, and John immediately grew concerned about her whereabouts. He questioned neighbors, friends, and local shopkeepers. While most people reported seeing her at her daily errands, no one reported anything unusual. Finally, John alerted her family, now living in the area, that she was missing. While the family seemed nonplussed by her disappearance, they did not appear overly concerned, which led John to believe they knew more than they were willing to share.

Undeterred by the lack of cooperation from his in-laws, John mounted a huge search for his wife. He spent many hours following leads. He placed large advertisements in the local newspapers. He hired the world famous Pinkerton Detective Agency to search for his wife. The agency claimed to have traced Barbara as far as New York City, but lost any sign of her, though they could offer no definitive proof that it was Barbara who boarded the *Day Liner* at Kingston Point that afternoon on her way to New York City. There were no pictures of Barbara and eyewitness testimony was only based on oral descriptions. Did Barbara run away? If she had, why had she left no note explaining her reasons?

John's business began to suffer as he spent more and more time away from the shop searching for his wife. His children needed care and he was having difficulties finding someone to come into his home and take care of them. In desperation he started to bring the children to his work. Blacksmith shops were no place for young children. John's youngest, Edward, walked behind a horse being fitted for new shoes. The horse spooked and kicked young Edward squarely in the back of the head. The boy suffered traumatic brain injuries. Though he survived, he grew up with the imprint of a horseshoe squarely on the back of his head and was permanently brain damaged.

A few years later, Sebastian, the oldest boy, could see his family falling apart. His father was tired and haggard, traveling often, looking for his missing wife.

The Brown's family burial plot in St. Mary's Cemetery, Kingston.
There family left space for Barbara in hopes of her return.

For the first time in their lives money was tight. Sebastian, believing he was a burden on the family, ran away and became a mule boy on the canal system. John was heartbroken when he learned his son had run away. In a moment of enlightenment, he realized that the search for his wife was ruining the rest of the family. Taking what was left of his fortune, he mounted a search for his son, finally locating him in Chicago.

He brought him home and decided that, while he would never stop searching for his wife, he must put his children first. He hired help in the house and returned to blacksmithing full time. So what became of Barbara Hartmann? John suspected that she did in fact "runaway," but no definitive proof was ever found. If her family knew something about her disappearance, they never gave any indication of where she might be. Had she been the victim of foul play?

While Barbara's family continued to remain silent about Barbara's disappearance, John found it difficult to believe that, if Barbara were alive, she never attempted any contact with her children. How could a mother of six simply abandon her children forever? When Mary died at age twenty in 1881, John hoped that his wife, if alive, would come forward to reunite with her other children. John went to his grave in 1888 not having one crumb of evidence to the whereabouts of his missing wife. However, the mystery continues. If Barbara had left because of her husband, and was still alive, why didn't she attempt contact with her surviving children after John's death? Each one of her children also went to their graves wondering about the reasons for their mother's disappearance.

An eternal optimist, I believe that if Barbara did leave on her own accord, there is still hope that someone has the missing piece to this intriguing puzzle. Maybe a family member, somewhere, remembers hearing this story and has the missing piece of this puzzle. What happened almost 150 years ago can't hurt anyone anymore but finding the solution to this intriguing puzzle could help answer the questions the family still harbors. Where is Barbara?

Missing Persons Report

MISSING

Judge Force Crater.
Courtesy of the Doe Network.

HAVE YOU SEEN THIS MAN?
Judge Joseph Force Crater

Race: White
Sex: Male
DOB: January 5, 1889
Last Seen: Outside of Billy Haas's Chophouse, West 45th Street, New York City.
Circumstances of Disappearance: Last seen leaving dinner and walking toward the theater district. If you know anything about the disappearance of Judge Joseph Force Crater, please contact the author at marianna.boncek@gmail.com or the Doe Network, c/o Todd Matthews, 121 Short Street, Livingston, TN 38570, or call 931-397-3893; their fax number is 931-823-9821 and their website is www.doenetwork.org.

MISSING

THE LOWELL SUN

de Two-Year Search Only Deepens
ery of Judge Crater's Disappearance

DESTROYS
PERS ON
DAY HE
PPEARS

DINES
WITH
FRIENDS

MRS STELLA
CRATER

SALLY
RITZ

DEPARTS
IN
TAXICAB
TO
OBLIVION

Two years and the expenditures of $300,000 by investigators has only deepened the fog of mystery that veils the

Sally Lou Ritz.
*Courtesy of the Doe
Network.*

HAVE YOU SEEN THIS WOMAN?

Sally Lou Ritz

Race: White
Sex: Female
Last Seen: September 1930
Circumstances of Disappearance: Unclear. If you know anything about Sally Lou Ritz, please contact the author at marianna.boncek@gmail.com or Doe Network, c/o Todd Matthews, 121 Short Street, Livingston, TN 38570; Phone: 931-397-3893

The Missingest Man in New York
and
Sally Lou Ritz

The disappearance of New York State Supreme Court Justice Joseph Force Crater is one of the most famous missing person cases of all times. However, the mention of his missing mistress, Sally Lou Ritz, is often just a passing footnote. Also, the details of the missing judge's disappearance have taken on mythic proportions. Newspapers, eager for news, printed rumors as facts, which then took on a life on their own. Much of what happened on the night of August 6, 1930, is open to speculation. Even though Judge Joseph Force Crater was a public man, his life was not an open book.

New York, on that hot summer night in 1930, was still riding high on the heels of the 1920s. Mobsters, corruption, and politicians all went hand-in-hand. Before his appointment to the bench, Joseph Crater was an up-and-coming lawyer. He was a Democrat and associated with the politics of Tammany Hall. Prior to being named judge, he was secretary to Senator Robert Wagner. He had not expected to be named by Governor Franklin D. Roosevelt to fill an unexpired term vacated by Judge Albert Vitale in the wake of a scandal, and there were hints that Joseph Crater may have "bought" his judgeship through the politicos of Tammany Hall. Just three months after Crater was appointed justice, front page news went wild about the possible scandal of judgeships being bought and sold. Surely, Judge Crater would have been called to testify in the scandal if he had not disappeared. Perhaps he had been involved in this scandal. However, because of his disappearance, this will forever be left to speculation.

Joe Crater liked living the high life. Though married, he earned the nickname "Good Time Joe." He was said to be fond of yachting, the theater, dining out, and dancing. He was known to do a little gambling and occasionally visiting mob-run establishments where patrons could order alcohol during prohibition. He also was very fond of women and reportedly had several mistresses. Despite all this, he was a well-liked and respected man.

Sally Lou Ritz's background is a bit murkier. She was a 22-year-old show girl (some reports claim she was as young as seventeen) when she went missing about a month after Crater's disappearance, though the date and place of her disappearance are just as murky as the girl herself. She was reportedly working as a show girl. Who reported her missing and when is also a mystery. According to early published reports, Crater dined with Mr. and Mrs. Ritz and their daughter, Sally Lou. Later accounts claim the diners were Crater, Sally Lou Ritz, and a lawyer, William Klein. The only thing constant in the two versions of this story is Sally Lou Ritz and Crater's disappearance.

Like most of New York's upper crust, the Craters did not spend the hot summer months in the city. They owned a summer home in Belgrade Lakes, Maine. After attending to some business in New York, Crater left for Maine on August 1, 1930, to join his wife, Stella, who was already relaxing at their home in Maine. Crater told neighbors he planned to stay at least two or three weeks and then head back to New York for the opening of what would be his first session on New York's Supreme Court. Once in Maine, Crater received a message that there was a phone call for him in town — the Craters had no phone in their house — and after coming home told his wife that he would have to return to New York to "straighten those fellows out." He told Stella he thought he'd be back on August 6, but, if matters took longer, he would definitely be back on August 9th to celebrate Stella's birthday.

When Crater returned to his apartment in New York, he told the maid she could return on August 7th, presumably because he would have left for Maine

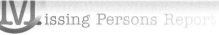

the previous evening, and that the Craters would not need her services again until August 25th — the day Crater was scheduled to start his session in court.

Nothing seemed too pressing on Crater's agenda, even though he had claimed to Stella that he was in New York to "straighten those fellows out." On Monday, August 4, Crater spent his morning working in his chambers. He had lunch at a nearby restaurant and visited his doctor. Previously, Crater had slammed his hand in a car door and one of his fingers was still injured from the incident. In the evening, he attended a show. After the show, Crater visited a club, reportedly mob-run, and then returned to his apartment. The next day, Tuesday, August 5, he lunched with some colleagues and later that night went to the house of some friends to play a little poker. Again, he returned home with nothing seemingly out of the ordinary.

On the morning of his disappearance, he returned to his chambers. This time he asked his assistant, Joseph Mara, to cash two checks and bring the money back to him. These checks totaled $5,150, a considerable sum in those days. When Mara returned, Crater asked for Mara's help in bringing some documents back to his apartment. Some of these documents would later be destroyed by the judge. When he left his office, Crater told both Mara and Fred Johnson, his law secretary, that he was going for a swim that afternoon. Crater belonged to a country club, but there is no record of his visit that day. Crater ate a late lunch at a nearby restaurant, attended to some more business, and then bought a single ticket to that evening's performance of *Dancing Partners*. Crater decided to dine that evening at Billy Haas's Chophouse located on West 45th Street in Manhattan.

According to reports, William Klein, a lawyer well-acquainted with Crater, and Sally Lou Ritz were dining together. Klein, seeing Crater enter, invited him to join them and he did. The trio left the restaurant well after the show *Dancing Partners* was scheduled to begin. At sometime around 9:15 p.m., the trio stood outside of the restaurant. In one report, Crater climbs into a waiting cab and Klein and Ritz walk off. In another report, Klein and Ritz enter the cab and

Missing Persons Report

Crater heads in the direction of the theater. Either way, outside of Billy Haas's Chophouse is the last time anyone has ever reportedly seen Judge Joseph Force Crater. His ticket for *Dancing Partners* was picked up at the box office, but no one can confirm it was Crater who retrieved the ticket and no one reportedly saw him at the show.

Also, no one immediately noticed Crater's disappearance. Everyone in New York thought he had left for Maine and everyone in Maine thought he was busy in New York. Stella sent someone to pick her husband up from the train on Thursday, August 7th, but he did not arrive. She was not worried; he said he'd be home by her birthday. When her birthday arrived and her husband had still not shown, Stella was more annoyed than worried. She thought business had kept him in the city through the weekend. After all, he was a newly appointed justice and was busy getting used to his responsibilities.

On Monday, August 11, Stella phoned New York. She spoke to Simon Rifkin, a friend of Crater's and the man who replaced Crater as law clerk for Senator Robert Wagner when Crater became a Justice. Rifkin assured Stella that he had, in fact, seen the judge when he really hadn't. Stella requested that Rifkin tell Crater to phone Stella. Rifkin reportedly never looked for his friend or called Stella back.

On August 15th, with no word from New York, Stella dispatched their chauffeur, Fred Kahler, to New York. He arrived on August 16th. Everything seemed in order in the Crater's Fifth Avenue apartment; however, Crater was not there and, based on the amount of mail that had piled up, had not been there in some time. However, Kahler also assured Stella that, even though he couldn't seem to locate the judge, others had seen him around.

On August 22nd, Kahler returned to Maine. This time he did not reassure Stella. He told her that he could not locate Crater and that Crater's associates discouraged him from actively making inquiries into the judge's apparent disappearance. Kahler said people didn't want him to give the judge any bad press and ruin his chances for re-election.

Judge Joseph Force Crater did not appear for the beginning of the Supreme Court term on August 25, 1930. Chief Judge Louis Valente called Stella in Maine with his concern. Still wanting to keep the disappearance quiet, some of Crater's associates instructed a former New York City detective to make some quiet inquiries. When the detective and Crater's assistant were denied access to the apartment, Stella finally thought it was time to act. She headed back to New York. She arrived on Friday, August 29. Reportedly, Stella hysterically called friends, none of whom had seen Crater. Stella also claims she carefully searched the apartment, finding that only the suit the judge last wore was missing. Unbelievably, she returned to Maine the next day.

The Judge's disappearance could no longer be kept quiet. Too many inquiries had been made and it was quite obvious he was missing from the bench. On September 3, 1930, almost a month since he was last seen, headlines blazed the news to all New York. For days after this initial report, the missing judge made the headlines. All of New York was abuzz with the news. Simon Rifkin, on learning of the headlines, called the police to report Crater missing on September 3rd. Strangely, Rifkin claimed that Crater had been murdered, though he could offer no clues as to who murdered the judge or where the judge's body could be found. On September 6th, Stella phoned the police, from Maine, to make a formal missing persons report. The police made a search of the Craters' New York apartment and found nothing out of the ordinary or any clue as to where the missing justice could be.

Rumors began to swirl immediately that Crater was linked romantically with several show girls; though many of these girls were questioned, none seemed to be able to shed any light on where Crater could be. Crater was "spotted" all over New York and the police followed leads all over the state. None could be substantiated.

On September 12th, Stella received a ransom note at her home in Maine demanding $20,000 for the safe return of her husband. The note had been mailed on

September 4th from New York. Police dismissed the letter as a hoax from some reader who had seen the story in the paper and was trying to cash in.

On September 15, 1930, a grand jury was convened to hear testimony into the disappearance of Judge Joseph Force Crater. A whole host of interesting people testified at Crater's inquiry; friends, show girls, politicos, even Supreme Court justices. Some testified that Crater ran off while others said he had been murdered. No one, though, was able to offer any proof of their assertions. While the grand jury testimony fueled new and interesting rumors and theories, it did nothing to forward the cause of the missing judge. The Grand Jury's preliminary ruling, coming early in November, was that there simply was not enough evidence to come to any conclusion about the judge's disappearance. Though the Grand Jury remained on-call until January 1931, no significant evidence was presented. Sometime after her grand jury testimony, Sally Lou Ritz simply disappeared.

Stella Crater stubbornly refused to return to New York. She refused to answer questions sent to her by the New York City police. She was becoming less and less cooperative. Because she was in Maine, she could not be subpoenaed by the New York State Courts. Finally, she did answer questions, in writing, sent to her by the District Attorney; however, her answers were far from helpful. She confined many of her responses to one or two words. Only when the grand jury investigation was formally closed, and she could no longer be called to testify, did Stella return home. She arrived in New York on January 18, 1931, four months after her husband's disappearance.

In a rather stunning discovery, Stella claimed to have found, tucked away in a bureau drawer, four manila envelopes addressed directly to Stella from her husband. In those envelopes, Stella found over $6,000 in cash, checks payable to the judge, bank books, a copy of the Judge's will, deeds for properties owned by the Craters, stock certificates, and a hand-written note of all the people Crater felt owed him money and the amount owed. The latest check was dated August 4th, before the judge's disappearance. Also scribbled

on the bottom of the note was a message, which was unclear. Some have read it as "*I am very weary*" while others claim it reads "*I am very sorry.*" Either way, the judge signed "*Love, Joe*" at the bottom of the paper. How had two police searches of the apartment failed to find these envelopes? How had Stella not previously found these envelopes on her first trip back to New York in August?

After revealing the contents of the envelopes to the authorities and claiming her husband was murdered for political reasons, Stella spent the winter in Florida. She went on to live a quiet life, and she always insisted that her husband had been murdered. She and her lawyer even presented their case to the courts in order for Stella to receive insurance payouts from her husband's life insurance policies. Eventually, Stella got a job, remarried, and even wrote a book about her husband's disappearance called *The Empty Robe*. In 1939, she had her husband declared legally dead. Stella died in 1969. The Craters had no children.

Since his disappearance, Judge Crater has been "seen" all over the world and in some unlikely situations: prospecting for gold on the Mexican border, farming in Canada, living in Cuba, not to mention lounging in many exotic places. However, not one credible shred of evidence has ever been put forward as to where the judge might be and what his fate was.

In 1956, inmate Camilio Weston Leyra was serving time in Sing Sing Prison for the vicious beating death of his parents. His conviction was later overturned and Leyra was freed when the Supreme Court ruled that his confession had been coerced. In a splashy tabloid style article coauthored by Richard Gehman, "I Know Who Killed Judge Crater!", which appeared in the September 16, 1956, edition of *The American Weekly*, Leyra claimed that another inmate, Harry Stein, confessed to having Judge Crater killed in a botched plot to extort money out of the judge. Not a shred of evidence could confirm or deny Leyra's story. However, Leyra waited until after Stein's execution to release the story to the papers.

issing Persons Report

Another interesting development in the case happened in 2005. The estate of Stella Ferucci-Good handed over letters written by the woman to authorities. In a letter marked "Do not open until my death," Ferrucci-Good claims her husband, Robert Good, and Charlie Burns, both New York City policemen and a cab driver, Frank Burns, Charlie's brother, killed Crater and buried him under the Boardwalk at Coney Island. Reportedly, Good and Burns were working for the mob. Several newspapers claimed that skeletal remains were found in that location during renovations in the 1950s, but, thus far, these claims have been unsubstantiated.

Sally Lou Ritz's disappearance is a little murkier. Newspaper reports claim, as late as the third week in September, that Sally, according to her mother, was spending some quiet time, away from the press, with family in Pennsylvania. After that, no one saw or heard from Sally again.

So, what happened to Judge Crater and Sally Lou Ritz? Did they slip away and live the rest of their lives in anonymity? Who called Crater in Maine and exactly who was he going to "straighten out"? Was Crater fleeing a brewing scandal? Did Judge Crater commit suicide, as his note might suggest? If so, what happened to Ritz? Or was Judge Crater killed in a mob hit and Ritz killed to keep her quiet? Is the disappearance of the two just a coincidence? Or are they linked? Why did Stella not cooperate with the investigation of her husband's disappearance? Did she know more than she was willing to say? Why did Rifkin and Stella both insist from the beginning that Crater had been murdered? Where is Judge Joseph Force Crater? Where is Sally Lou Ritz?

issing Persons Report

MISSING

Richard Cox.
USMA Library.

HAVE YOU SEEN THIS MAN?
Richard Cox

Race: White
Sex: Male
DOB: July 25, 1928
Last Seen: January 14, 1950, a little after 6 p.m. on the parade grounds of the
West Point Military Academy.
Circumstances of Disappearance: Richard Cox was last seen walking to dinner
at the Thayer Hotel with a mysterious friend he called "George," who he had
claimed to serve with in Germany. If you know anything about Richard Cox
contact: the author at marianna.boncek@gmail.com or Doe Network c/o
Todd Matthews, 121 Short Street, Livingston, TN 38570, 931-397-3893

Richard Cox

When you first enter the grounds of the United States Military Academy at West Point, the aura of austerity and grandeur hits you simultaneously. Nothing is out of place on the grounds. Even the leaves that fall from the trees seemed purposely placed. The gray and black granite buildings are stolid and the grounds are immaculate. The campus sits high on a bluff and commands a breathtaking view of the Hudson River.

The United State Military Academy at West Point, sometimes simply referred by locals as "West Point," was established in 1802 to train officers for the country's new army. However, the military history of West Point goes back before the Revolutionary War. Here on the grounds of the Academy is where Benedict Arnold betrayed his country and fled. Also, from the shores, the great chain was stretched across the Hudson River to stop the advancing British Army in the Revolutionary War. Famous graduates of West Point include Robert E. Lee, George Armstrong Custer, Ulysses S. Grant, and Dwight D. Eisenhower. West Point has graduated astronauts, presidents, generals, business leaders, and war heroes. West Point has become synonymous with success.

A young man or woman chooses West Point because he or she wants a career in the military. Admission into the academy is competitive and future cadets must meet rigorous admission policies and also be nominated by a Congressman. Once admitted, the cadets face rigorous training, both physically and academically. Cadets are bound by a strict honor code,

which states that the cadets "will not lie, cheat, or steal or tolerate those that do." Cadets who break the honor code must have a hearing and if they are found guilty, they risk expulsion from the academy.

Not all cadets join the corps directly out of high school. Each year soldiers already serving our country apply and are accepted into the Corp. The process is the same for both active military personnel and new high school graduates — they all must meet the same admission criteria. This was the case with Richard Cox when he was accepted into West Point in 1948 after serving in active duty.

Richard Cox grew up in Mansfield, Ohio. He was the youngest in a family of six children. He was a smart, well-liked young man. After graduation from high school in 1946, Cox enrolled in the Army. Richard Cox seemed to achieve excellence in anything he chose to do. Cox served in the 28th Constabulary Unit in Germany. Men for this unit were handpicked by Major General Earnest Harmon. They were top-of-the-line soldiers. Here Cox would perform patrols on the border between East and West Germany. He served as an intelligence officer, which has led to rumors about his service and gives a mysterious aura to his background. However, nothing in his training and background suggests that he served at any high level in the intelligence service.

After two years of exemplary duty in the service, he applied to West Point and his application was fast-tracked. He excelled at West Point, performing in the top third of his class. He was on his way to a brilliant military career…and then he disappeared.

In the late afternoon of January 7, 1950, Cox received a phone call at his dormitory. Cadets do not have phones in their rooms so the call was answered by the cadet in charge of quarters. He told the caller that Cox was not in his room. The man left a message for Cox to meet him at the Thayer Hotel; a hotel located on the West Point campus grounds and is open to the public. The caller said that his name was "George" and he and Cox had served together in Germany.

Cox received the message and signed out to go visit his friend. "George" met Cox at the visitor's

center and, according to Cox, the two sat in George's car and drank. Cox returned to his room inebriated. This is where the mystery begins. Cox signed out at 18:23 (6:23 p.m.) It wasn't discovered until years after Cox went missing that the sign out book had been altered to 19:23, an hour later than Cox actually left campus. Did Cox want to mislead people to believe he had been at the cadet supper formation? Why would he want people to believe that he left campus an hour later than he had? If Cox had altered the sign out book, it was a clear violation of the cadet honor code. Why would Cox risk his future for a one hour sign out time that didn't make any difference? Did someone else alter the sign out book and if so, for what possible reason?

When Cox returned, his roommates were amused at his obvious drunkenness. Cox fell asleep at his desk while trying to study and one of his roommates playfully snapped a picture. They had never seen the older, more serious Cox in such a state. In an odd display, which the roommates attributed to his drunkenness, Cox awoke from his stupor, ran out into the hall, and called unintelligibly over the banister. What or who could make Cox behave so out of character?

George visited Cox the next day and, while several people saw George with Cox, none of them had a conversation with him. Cox mentioned his friend a few times in the following week, but never by name. Cox claimed the two had served together and that George was an admitted murderer. This mysterious visitor, according to Cox, had told a story of getting a young German girl pregnant and then murdering her and getting away with it. Cox's roommates weren't sure what to make of these stories and took them, at the time, as soldier's brag, nothing else.

The following Saturday, January 14, 1950, "George" returned for another visit with Cox, who signed out around 6 p.m., indicating that he and George were headed for supper at the Hotel Thayer. The last time anyone saw Richard Cox, he was walking across campus, a little after 6 p.m., with this mysterious visitor.

It was noticed quickly that Richard Cox had not returned from dinner. Cadets had to sign in, lights out, and rooms inspected. Just a little after 1 a.m. in the early morning of Sunday, January 15, everyone was signed in except for Cox. His roommates were worried. Cox's absence was reported. At 7:15 a.m., when it was daylight and clear out, there was no sign of the cadet. A search began. Searches of the dormitory were made and officers began to line up other cadets for questioning. They knew that this serious cadet was just not somewhere "sleeping it off." Late morning a call was placed to his family in Ohio informing them of Cox's disappearance and a request for any clues to his whereabouts. His family was shocked and could give no information about where Cox might be.

By mid-afternoon, Cox's classmates all knew of his strange disappearance and began their own search of the grounds. No one recalled seeing Cox at the Thayer Hotel and security could recall no one fitting Cox's description leaving the grounds. On Monday, an official and exhaustive search was done of all the installations, buildings, and grounds. Not one clue was found. By now, the local police were involved. They checked all hotels, motels, and lodgings for anyone fitting "George's" description, but the management at these places didn't recall anyone fitting that description renting a room.

Of course, rumors began to emerge about the bright, young cadet's disappearance…all of them unfounded. Some claimed he was a homosexual and fled the army to live in New York City. Others claimed he was recruited by the newly forming Central Intelligence Agency. Cox's family categorically denies all of these rumors — he was a serious student and would never voluntarily disappear without contacting them.

The search for Richard Cox was wide and extensive. Strangely, according to Harry Maihafter in his book *Oblivion: The Mystery of the West Point Cadet Richard Cox*, in 1952 a witness, Ernest Shotwell, claimed he saw and spoke with Cox at a restaurant in Washington, D.C. Shotwell had known Cox from spending time in a preparatory program for entrance into West Point. Shotwell had not satisfactorily

completed the program and was unable to attend West Point. Shotwell claimed he called Cox by name, though Cox did not address him by name. Shotwell said Cox seemed cold and distracted. He asked Cox about the academy and Cox told Shotwell he had resigned from the academy. The conversation was short, less than five minutes. Shotwell was not aware, until two years later in 1954, that Cox was missing. At that time, he came forward with his story. Was this really Richard Cox? Or someone who just looked like Cox and made small talk with a stranger? Extensive investigation could not confirm or deny that the man Shotwell saw in the restaurant was Cox.

Cox's "friend," George, has never been identified. Cox did not serve with a man named George in Germany. So, who is he and was he involved in Cox's disappearance? Did Cox have some damaging information on George's activities and did George murder him to silence him? Did Cox run away? Where is Richard Cox?

MISSING

Freddie "Tookie" Holmes. *Courtesy of Dorothy Brown.*

HAVE YOU SEEN THIS MAN?
Freddie "Tookie" Holmes

Race: White
Sex: Male
DOB: July 2, 1953
Weight: 30 lbs.
Eyes: Blue Eyes
Last Seen: Denman Mountain Road, Grahamsville, 9:00 a.m.
Circumstances of Disappearance: Freddie was last seen by his mother walking down the driveway of his home at approximately 9 a.m. in Grahamsville, New York, on May 25, 1955. In spite of a massive search of approximately 1,000 people, including police, firemen, volunteers, a bloodhound, and a helicopter, no sign of the boy has ever been found. If you have any information regarding Freddie Holmes, contact the Sullivan County Sheriff's Office at 845-794-7100.

issing Persons Report

Freddie "Tookie" Holmes

In 1955, life was simpler and slower than it is today. Most country people took their lives in stride. They tended little gardens, made all their food from scratch, and lived the best they could on very little. High up in the Catskills, there was little or no television reception, so families read, did work around the house, and the children played outside for hours. The Holmes were no different. The farmhouse they rented was located high up on Denman Mountain Road in the little hamlet of Grahamsville. The road past their house was a one-lane dirt road. They had no neighbors. Times were tough. Sometimes it seemed that there wasn't enough to spread out at the table with eight children, but there was always enough love. Roderick went to work with the highway department each day, the children went to school, and Gertrude tended to the house and garden.

On the morning of May 25, 1955, with the last of the spring frost finally gone, Gertrude Holmes was putting in her garden. Forecast predicted rain in the coming days and she wanted to make sure everything was in before the rain arrived. Freddie was a beautiful baby; just two months shy of his second birthday. He had golden blonde curly hair. His family affectionately called him "Tookie." He played out in the garden as his mother worked on her hands and knees. She had him dressed for the cool weather in brown corduroy coveralls and a long-sleeve polo search. Freddie toddled down to the shed where the landlord, Baldassare Garizzio, was working.

The rural, one-lane road that runs in front of Freddie Holmes' house. The road is now paved. At the time of his disappearance, it was a dirt road.

Garizzio was a cobbler from Brooklyn and he and his wife often stayed with the Holmes family during their visits to the country. He kept a locked garage on the property. Garizzio once had told Freddie's mother that Freddie was such a gorgeous child someone would pay a lot of money for him.

Freddie stopped and looked into the doorway where Garizzio was working. According to Garizzio, he spoke to the little boy and then Freddie toddled off. This was the last time anyone has ever seen Freddie. After a short while, his mother stood up and called to the boy. There was no answer. Unconcerned, she started a cursory search. She couldn't find him. The landlord recounted seeing him, but did not know which way he had gone. His mother's concern started to grow. Calling loudly, she began to look everywhere: under porches, in the shed, around the yard... Freddie was gone.

Gertrude called neighbors to see if perhaps, as unlikely as it was since the nearest house was a mile away, Freddie had toddled off for a visit. As concern turned to panic, neighbors and friends joined in the search. By the time the police received a call and the first car came to the remote location, night was beginning to fall. Siblings and family had been searching all afternoon, but any comprehensive search would take place the following day. One of the largest searches in Sullivan County history was about to commence.

More than 1,000 searchers joined the effort. The community immediately rallied around the Holmes family. School was cancelled the following day so teachers and students alike could aid in the search. Police agencies from Sullivan, Delaware, and Ulster Counties sent searchers. The Woodbourne Civil Defense organizations and prison guards from the Woodbourne Prison joined the search. Volunteer firemen from Grahamsville, Liberty, Hurleyville, Fallsburg, Woodridge, White Sulphur Springs, Woodbourne, Neversink, and Monticello left their jobs and farms to assist in the search. Search dogs and their handlers arrived. Even a helicopter from Stewart Air Force Base joined in. Heavy rains began to fall,

hampering the search. The dogs picked up a scent and then lost it near the road. Shoulder to shoulder, in the pouring rain, searchers worked tirelessly. After three days, not one sign was found of the boy; not a shoe, a button, or a footprint. Slowly, friends and neighbors returned to their work and suspicion focused on the family.

Gertrude and Roderick were taken to Albany, an almost three-hour trip in those days, for a polygraph test. They passed. Each of the six older children were brought into separate rooms, away from their parents, and asked questions such as, "Did your parents ever hit you?" They were all scared and confused. Gertrude told investigators that earlier in the morning she had seen a strange car pass by on the dirt road outside their home.

Gertrude's newly planted garden was dug up and the floorboards of the outbuildings were ripped up. It was clear that the authorities were looking for a body, though they continued to insist there was no sign of foul play. Search warrants were requested for all the neighboring homes, and over the next few months, every inch of the mountain that could be searched was and then some.

To complicate matters, a few days after Freddie went missing, investigators discovered stolen items in Garizzio's locked garage, such as tools and chainsaws taken from neighboring farms. They also discovered Communist literature, books, and pamphlets hidden away in the garage. Searchers became so angry they decided on vigilante justice and there was talk about lynching Garizzio. Luckily for Garizzio's safety, the police arrested him. Even though there was no evidence of Garizzio being involved in Freddie's disappearance, suspicion immediately fell on him.

After three days of intensive search, the search parties began to dissipate. People returned to the business of their regular lives. The Holmes family tried to carry on. It wasn't easy. Every so often the police arrived on their doorstep armed with pictures of dead boys for the family to look at. It was a difficult process. To deal with the pain, Roderick turned to drinking heavily and thirteen years after his son's disappearance he committed suicide not far from where his son went missing. Gertrude died suddenly at age 61. Her family believed she died of a broken heart. Car accidents and illness took six of Freddie's sibling (one born after his death) to early graves, leaving only two sisters alive. They continue their tireless search.

What happened to Freddie? Did he wander off, fall in a crevice, or get taken by a wild animal? If so, why haven't the remains of his clothing ever been located? Was he kidnapped and sold? If so, how was he taken from this remote area unseen? Did the kidnapper have an accomplices hidden in the heavily wooded area? Was Garizzio involved in the boy's disappearance? Where is Freddie?

Missing Persons Report

MISSING

John Lake.
Courtesy of Eric Lake.

HAVE YOU SEEN THIS MAN?
John Lake

Race: White
Sex: Male
DOB: February 18, 1930
Age At Disappearance: 37
Height: 6'0"
Weight: 180 lbs.
Last Seen: On the sidewalk in midtown Manhattan headed back to his apartment on Christopher Street. If you know anything about John Lake, contact the author at marianna.boncek@gmail.com or the Doe Network, c/o Todd Matthews, 121 Short Street, Livingston, TN 38570, or call 931-397-3893; fax: 931-823-9821, website: www.doenetwork.org.

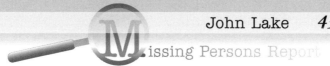
John Lake

Eric Lake describes the memories of his father as fleeting, brief still life moments that are not connected in any sort of pattern. Eric had just turned six years old when his dad, John Lake, a sports editor for *Newsweek*, went missing from Greenwich Village in Manhattan. His parents had been separated on and off and were finally headed for divorce, but the memories in Eric's mind are not the bitter end. Rather, he remembers arguing with his sister, two years his senior, about who would sit next to dad at breakfast. He remembers his father bouncing him on the bed and a fleeting memory of a Columbia College football game, but that is all. Eric would grow up with a deep sense of loss, an emotion he describes as shame, from his father's disappearance. Over forty-four years later, Eric still wonders where his father is.

John Lake was a serious, book smart sort of man. Born in Albany, New York, in 1930, like most children of this generation, he was raised with discipline and hard work. He was known as a serious and studious boy who was a natural in athletics. After his graduation from high school, he attended Syracuse University on scholarship to study journalism. In Syracuse, he began his career as a journalist with *The Daily Orange*. Lake enlisted in the Navy, and served from 1951-1955. While in Hawaii, he carried on a long-distance love affair with Alice, who would later become his wife.

After marrying in Hawaii, the Lakes settled in Syracuse, but soon left to enable John to pursue his journalism career in Binghamton. He eventually found his way to New York City where he ended up as sports editor for *Newsweek*. He quickly became a well-respected and award-winning journalist.

Unfortunately, as his career was taking off, his marriage was falling apart. After two separations and trial reconciliations, the Lakes started living apart; Alice Lake and the children were living in New Jersey and John rented an apartment on Christopher Street in Manhattan. Lake was struggling financially and had been feeling restless. Some claim he was feeling a bit out of sorts, even a bit depressed, in the days leading up to his disappearance. On Saturday, December 11, 1967, John missed an important interview with Jim Schaaf from the football team, the Kansas City Chiefs. This was out-of-character for him, as he took his job very seriously and would never miss such an important interview. Later, people would wonder if this was a harbinger of his disappearance or just a coincidence.

It was Sunday, December 10, 1967, Lake was feeling a bit lonely and called several friends for dinner. His on-again/off-again girlfriend, Jean, was out of town. Everyone was busy. He finally ended up calling a friend of a friend, named Sandy, who initially declined a dinner date, but finally accepted when Lake called her back a second time. They dined at a restaurant called La Poette. According to Sandy, Lake became quite inebriated as the evening went on. Lake accompanied her to her apartment. According to Sandy, she had an early morning the next day and did not invite Lake up to her place. Lake left on foot to head home. It is unclear if he planned on grabbing the subway back or walking the entire way to his own apartment, which would not have been unusual for Lake. No one has seen John Lake since.

John Lake. *Courtesy of Eric Lake.*

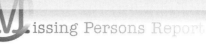

His disappearance was not noticed immediately. Since the magazine was "put to bed" on Saturday nights, no one expected Lake in the office on Monday. He sometimes came to the office on Tuesdays and sometimes he didn't, so Tuesday came and went without anyone noticing anything out of the ordinary. It was only on Wednesday; Lake's boss asked where he was. Jean, Lake's girlfriend, was also a co-worker and she was sent to Lake's apartment to see what was up. Jean came back and reported that no one answered the door. After his co-workers made a few phone calls, they knew something was out of the ordinary. It was then that Lake's boss called his wife. Alice knew right away something was wrong.

Alice made phone calls to friends. Finally, she called the police and was told she would need to make the missing person's report in person. She traveled into the city and made the report. John Lake had been missing seventy-two hours when the report was taken. Later, Alice and a neighbor convinced the police to let them into Lake's apartment. Since John had just moved in, there was still a disarray of unpacked boxes; it was hard to tell if he had made it back to his apartment Sunday night. The police never searched Lake's apartment.

Eventually, Alice would pack up her husband's apartment and take the few belongings back to New Jersey with her. Without the rent being paid, the landlord required the apartment to be empty by the end of December. In his belongings, Alice found tickets to the show "Brigadoon" on December 27th. Since it was Lake's favorite show; Alice went there hoping that John would show up. He did not. The search for Lake simply petered out. The police did no formal investigation. Some people thought that John, stressed by his marital and financial problems, just left town. Others thought he might have taken his own life. The family hired the famous Pinkerton Detective Agency. They were not able to shed any light into the disappearance of John Lake. Days, months, and eventually years went by, but no one heard anything from John Lake.

Eric grew up and eventually, their mother moved the family to a small town in Maine. Eric continued to wonder what happened to his father. Eric Lake has carried out an intensive investigation of his father's disappearance. He has left no stone unturned. He has found no clues to his father's whereabouts. Where is John Lake?

Age progression of John Lake.
Courtesy of Eric Lake.

MISSING

Michael Alfinito.
Courtesy of Susan Alfinito.

HAVE YOU SEEN THIS MAN?
Michael Alfinito

Race: White
Sex: Male
DOB: May 20, 1956
Weight: 180 lbs
Eyes: Brown
Hair: Reddish brown
Last Seen: March 25, 1984, at his apartment in Bayside, Queens. If you know anything about Michael Alfinito, please contact the New York City Police Department at (212) 694-7781.

Michael Alfinito

Susan Alfinito and her family vacation each year at the same resort in Pennsylvania. One year, the owners hired a drifter to do maintenance work around the resort. Susan remembers looking really closely at him to see if he was, in fact, her missing brother, Michael. He wasn't, but that is how the families of the missing live.

Michael Alfinito was just twenty-seven years old when he disappeared without a trace. He was tall, handsome, with bushy reddish-brown hair. He was athletic, enjoyed body-building, and worked for Jack LaLanne, a fitness expert and body builder. He was the only boy in his family of four siblings. His sisters adored him.

Michael had spent most of his early adult life as a "roadie," traveling around with bands, such as Joan Jett and Hall and Oates. However, love had different plans for Michael. He met a woman and they fell deeply in love. She asked him to leave the road so they could build a life together and he agreed. He decided he would switch careers and become an EMT. He was working toward that goal when he disappeared.

Being on the road had been difficult for Michael. He had financial difficulties and was forced to borrow money from family and friends, but things seemed to be coming together for him. However, Michael got devastating news just before he disappeared. The woman he changed his life for decided she wanted to break up.

On Sunday, March 24, 1985, Michael's sister, Susan, called him to invite him for dinner. She knew he was struggling and thought being with family would help. Michael said he was too busy, no matter how adamantly she tried to get him to join them. He promised her he would stop by soon for a visit. That night, Michael reportedly went over to his friend Louie's house for some drinks. Louie said Michael left in the early hours of Monday, March 25.

Susan called her brother two days later to check on him. She got his answering machine and left a message. Another sister had tried reaching her brother and had also left a message. Five days later, after no one had heard from Michael, Susan and her sister decided to go to his apartment in Bayside, Queens, to check on him. When they arrived, the door to his apartment was ajar. They went in. Dirty dishes were in the sink and when they checked the refrigerator, the milk was expired. The place looked like Michael had not been there in some while. The sisters called their father who arrived shortly. They could find no clue of where Michael was so they called friends. When Susan reached Louie, he told Susan he had something to tell her in person. However, when Louie arrived at Michael's apartment and saw the family gathered there, he suddenly had nothing to add to what he had already told Susan — that Michael had been at his apartment the Monday before.

The Alfinitos called the police to report Michael missing. He had been missing for almost five days by the time the police report was filed. During their investigation, the police discovered that Louie had possession of Michael's car. When asked how he came to have the car, he explained that Michael owed him money, so he gave Louie the car. While suspicious, the story was plausible. Michael had gotten himself in a lot of debt and owed many people money. However, he had not transferred the title to Louie. This struck Michael's sister as odd, but possession of Michael's car did not mean that Louie had been involved in Michael's disappearance. It seemed as if Michael had simply stepped off the face of the earth.

A few weeks later, Susan suddenly remembered reading a story of a man, fitting Michael's description,

jumping from the Staten Island Ferry in a suicide attempt. Could this have been Michael? Had he been more distraught about his break-up and financial problems than she had thought? This body has never been recovered.

Years later, Susan was on the computer, as she often is, looking for clues about her brother's disappearance. She was looking at the FBI website for unidentified remains. Forensic artists recreate what a person might have looked like in life using unidentified skeletal remains. She came upon a reconstruction that she thought looked very much like her brother. The skeletal remains of a man fitting Michael's description had been found in New Jersey. He had been murdered. However, the reconstructed face of a man had black hair, her brother had red. She contacted the artist and he told her that the skeletal remains could have had red hair. She then contacted authorities to have her DNA checked against that of the remains. The remains had been found in New Jersey; therefore, the New Jersey State Police were contacted. In a surprising twist, Susan was told that the New Jersey police had lost the remains! Susan was devastated.

The forensic artist, however, still had the skull. Three attempts were made to extract a DNA sample from the teeth, but they all failed. Finally, Susan asked for an examination of the dental records. In another devastating twist, the New York Police Department had lost Michael's dental records and Michael's dentist had long since destroyed records. Dentists are not required to keep dental records of inactive patients for more than seven years. The skull was sent to a forensic lab in Texas. A year later, the FBI contacted Susan to tell her that the remains were not, in fact, her brother Michael. Susan has her doubts.

What happened to Michael? Is the body the New Jersey State Police lost actually Michael's? Did he jump off the Staten Island ferry in a state of depression? Does Louie know where Michael may have gone? Did something more sinister happen to Michael? Where is Michael?

Missing Persons Report

MISSING

Petra Muhammad. *Courtesy of the Doe Network.*

HAVE YOU SEEN THIS WOMAN?

Petra Loretta Boatswain Muhammad

Race: Black
Sex: Female
Eyes: Brown
Hair: Brown
Last Seen: January 7, 2006, outside of her home in on Schneider Avenue in Highland Falls around 3 p.m. If you know anything about Petra Muhammad, please contact the Highland Falls Police at 845-446-4911.

Petra Loretta Boatswain Muhammad

Though you would never know it from her cheerfulness and determination, Petra Muhammad's life did not begin easily. Petra was born in Grenada and was adopted by her family as an infant. She spent her childhood years in the care of different relatives. At fourteen, she moved to Trinidad. When she was twenty-two, she went on vacation to New York City and met her future husband, William Jackson, who would later change his last name to Muhammad when he converted to Islam. William was a kind, considerate man, who, like Petra, wanted to wait until marriage to begin a sexual relationship. Petra was smitten with him and his old-fashioned values. Petra returned to Trinidad, but could not get the handsome man out of her mind. Two years later she returned to New York and married William. They moved to Highland Falls, near William's family, to start their life together. Petra was thrilled. She was finally going to have the close, loving family she always wanted.

A year after their marriage, Petra became pregnant. It was a difficult pregnancy. William was now working in Washington, D.C., leaving his wife in Highland Falls. As the pregnancy progressed, Petra had to be hospitalized due to complications. Her husband was not there for support. The couple began to bicker and the marriage started to show serious signs of strain. William was becoming angrier and Petra was feeling emotionally abandoned. Petra began visiting her family in the Bronx and, during these visits, would complain about her husband. Petra claimed he was becoming abusive. Back together in

Highland Falls, after the baby was born, Petra claimed things got even worse. The couple finally decided to throw in the towel and, in July 2005, William filed for divorce. In September, Petra followed suit and requested an order of protection from her husband. She claimed that her husband had abused their child and threatened to kill her. She testified in court that William had told her he hadn't killed her yet because he couldn't find a place to dispose of her body. While both agreed they wanted the divorce, the point of contention became the couple's son. They both wanted full custody. William wanted to raise his son as a true and faithful Muslim. Petra claimed her husband wanted to raise her son as a bigot and train him to "kill white people."

While the divorce and custody fight plodded forward, Petra began to put her life back together. She got a job, part-time, at the United States Military Academy at West Point as a cashier. She signed up for classes at the local community college. She found an apartment and planned to meet the landlord to sign the lease. Once her divorce was finalized, Petra felt her life could finally move in the right direction.

On January 11, 2006, the Muhammads had a court date regarding their divorce, but neither of them showed up. The case was rescheduled to January 24th. On January 24, 2006, neither of the Muhammads again showed up for their day in divorce court. No one realized at this time, but Petra had already been missing for almost two weeks. William had not filed a missing person's report. The judge dismissed the case. On February 24, 2006, Petra missed a family court date regarding harassment charges she leveled against her husband. Even though no one showed, the judge ordered Child Protective Services to check on the welfare of the child.

It slowly became evident to family members in the Bronx they had not heard from Petra in awhile. They tried to contact her. Concerned, they called the police to do a welfare check. That last time anyone remembered seeing Petra was on January 7, 2006.

She had paid some bills, visited the mall, and was seen by a relative entering the house she still shared with William.

When the police questioned William, he said he had no idea where his wife was. He assumed she had finally taken off for good. He did not report her missing because he didn't realize she was missing. After all, they were in the middle of a contentious divorce and he just assumed she finally got her own place and moved on. The disturbing point, however, was that Petra left behind her son and all of her belongings. If she was "moving on," wouldn't she have taken her personal belongings with her? Wouldn't she have taken her son? Why would she miss the court dates that would have freed her from William and defined the custody arrangement?

The police conducted an extensive search in March 2006 in the home the Muhammads shared. Nothing suggesting Petra's whereabouts was found. However, the police found a doll in Petra's seat in the kitchen with a noose around its neck. As to date, the police have followed hundreds of leads and searched extensively for Petra. Not one clue to whereabouts has been found.

Why didn't Petra show up for her court dates? Why didn't William show up for his court dates? Did he know that Petra would also not show and the case would be dismissed? If Petra left the country, why hasn't she contacted anyone as to where she is? Where is Petra?

Missing Persons Report

MISSING

Kellisue Ackernecht.
Courtesy of Kalli Lee.

HAVE YOU SEEN THIS WOMAN?
Kellisue Ackernecht

Race: White
Sex: Female
DOB: December 16, 1972
Height: 5'10"
Weight: 135
Eyes: Brown
Hair: Brown
Last Seen: September 30, 2008, 9:45 p.m. leaving Rite-Aid Pharmacy in Amsterdam
Circumstances of Disappearance: Kellisue was last seen September 30th leaving her job as a shift supervisor at an Amsterdam Rite Aid around 9:45 p.m. She was driving a ten-year-old Saturn sedan. Three hours later, police found the car engulfed in flames a few blocks from her Johnstown home, with no sign of Kellisue. The car was parked in an area neighbors call Frog Hollow, near the Rail Trail. The car was completely destroyed by the fire. If you know anything about Kellisue Ackernecht, please contact the City of Johnstown Police at (518) 736-4021.

Kellisue Ackernecht

Not everyone's life is easy. Not all of us have someone to love and nurture us. Kellisue Ackernecht was born into a difficult situation. Her childhood was marked by difficulty. Social services intervened in her early childhood and one of her siblings was removed from the home. She struggled in school. Despite all this, most people described her as cheerful and confident. She made her way the best she could in the world and was well-liked. Eventually, she married. She met her husband, Jayson, while working at a local Burger King. They had a daughter, Ashley. Kellisue was active in the local fire department and her daughter's PTA. She had worked as a teacher's aide. She left that job and in September 2008 and found a job working in a local Rite Aid pharmacy. She took care of her daughter, liked to crochet, and smiled at her customers. She was an average person, like most of us, taking care of her family and making her way through life. Her disappearance almost went unnoticed.

Unfortunately, her marriage had begun to show signs of strain. Her husband, Jayson wasn't working due to disability. This dashed the dreams of Kellisue and Jayson getting their own home and moving out of his parents' home. With stress mounting, Kellisue had started an extra marital relationship with a local man, Matt Wrobel. At that time, Matt Wrobel lived in Gloversville, a short drive from Johnstown. Wrobel lived with his girlfriend and her children.

Kellisue was last seen September 30, 2008, in Amsterdam leaving her job as a shift supervisor at Rite

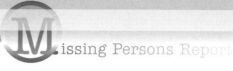

Aid Pharmacy around 9:45 p.m. She walked to her car with a co-worker. Her co-workers noted nothing out of the ordinary. She climbed into her car, a 1998 Saturn, and drove into oblivion.

Four hours later, the police, on a routine patrol, found Kellisue's car engulfed in flames about a quarter of a mile from her home. The call to the fire department was logged at 1:53 a.m. on October 1, 2008. The car was parked in an area neighbors call Frog Hollow, near a popular rail trail used for hiking and biking. The rail trail runs behind the homes on the street directly passed the home Kellisue shared with her husband, daughter, and in-laws. Someone could easily have left the area, via the rail trail, and be undetected. There was no sign of Kellisue anywhere. Kellisue was not in the car and the car and its contents were completely destroyed by the fire. The police could not determine the cause of the fire, but it started in the engine and is considered arson.

After discovering the car, the police traced the license plate and went to Kellisue's home. They woke her husband, Jayson, who was surprised that his wife was not yet home. Jayson allowed the police to search his home, property, and vehicles. Nothing out of the ordinary was found. At daybreak, a search helicopter took to the air for any signs of Kellisue.

On the night of the disappearance, one neighbor claimed to have heard a woman screaming. Another woman claimed to have heard two gunshots. The second woman woke at 12:15 a.m. to what she believed was a gunshot. Fifteen minutes later she awoke again to what she described as a second gunshot. She claims she looked out the window and did not see any fire; rather, she claimed to see car headlights where Kellisue's car was found later engulfed in flames. Though the witness claimed not to see any fire, the police dismissed the report of gunshots as tires or the gas tank from the Saturn exploding from the heat. The neighbor whose house is directly next to where Kellisue's car was found claimed he had been on his porch until 12:30 a.m. and heard and saw nothing out of the ordinary. His porch faces directly where Kellisue's car was found.

Almost two years later the burn area where Kellisue Ackernecht's car was found ablaze by police.

Kellisue Ackernecht's home. The entrance to the rail trail can be seen next to the house.

Initially, family and friends thought Kellisue might have chosen to disappear. After all, she was having an affair, disappointed in her marriage, and her husband claimed she was taking medication for depression. Maybe she just got tired of her life. Wrobel was located and questioned extensively to see if he had any plans with Kellisue the evening she disappeared or if he might have any clues to her whereabouts. After questioning Wrobel, police believed he had nothing to do with Kellisue's disappearance. He later moved out of the area. Also, most of her family and friends believe she would not have runaway and leave her daughter behind. The night she disappeared was just a week short of her daughter's birthday.

As the weeks wore on, searchers with cadaver dogs scoured the area. They found nothing. The case for Kellisue was going cold. It was about this time, Kalli J. Lee, a local mom, was reading the paper. Lee's daughter had been diagnosed with leukemia and the community had given her so much in the way of support, both financially and emotionally, she had been looking for a way to give back. Volunteering to help with the search for Kellisue was something she felt she could do. At first, the family welcomed Lee's involvement in the search. The family was feeling overwhelmed and confused, so it was nice to have someone help them out when they didn't know what to do.

After a short time, however, Lee realized that her efforts to keep Kellisue's story alive were being thwarted. If Lee put up missing posters, they were quickly torn down. Money Lee raised did not make it in the hands of searchers. She began to receive threatening phone calls. One time, Lee planned a vigil for Kellisue and called the press to attend. Mysteriously, the press received calls that the vigil had been canceled and, therefore, they did not attend. Jayson Ackernecht and his family stopped participating in searches and fund-raising. A rift began to form between Kellisue's family and her husband's family. However, this did not dissuade

Lee. It actually strengthened her resolve to help bring Kellisue home. Lee works hard with Kellisue's brother, Tom Kilcullen, in the search for Kellisue.

In Johnstown, Kalli Lee describes her search for Kellisue as a near obsession. She says that everyday she asks herself what can be done to bring Kellisue home. She maintains a website, a Facebook page, and works tirelessly to organize efforts to keep Kellisue's story alive. Lee says she gets angry when people ask her if Kellisue is still missing. Lee does everything in her power to keep Kellisue's story alive. She believes that Kellisue will be found. Where is Kellisue?

MISSING

Suzanne Lyall.
*Courtesy of Joe and
Mary Lyall.*

HAVE YOU SEEN THIS WOMAN?
Suzanne Lyall

Race: White
Sex: Female
DOB: April 6, 1978
Height: 5'3"
Weight: 175 lbs
Eyes: Blue Eyes
Hair: Blonde
Last Seen: March 2, 1998, at Crossgates Mall Albany, around 9 p.m., leaving
work at Babbages (located inside the mall). Possible sighting at 9:45 p.m.
Collin's Circle at the State University of Albany getting off the bus outside
her dorm. If you have any information about Suzanne Lyall, please contact
the New York State Police at 800-920-4150.

Suzanne Lyall

Just by looking at some people, you know that you are looking at someone special. Suzanne Lyall was like that. Suzanne had a wide impish grin and sparkling eyes. She had stunning thick strawberry-blonde hair that hung to the middle of her back. She usually wore a long black trench coat, the style in 1998, setting off a stunning contrast with her hair. She was noticeable. She wasn't someone who blended into the crowd.

Suzanne was a typical college sophomore at the State University at Albany. She worked part-time, had a boyfriend, and chatted on the computer in her spare time. She studied hard and received good grades. Her family affectionately calls her Suzy. She talked often on the phone with her mother. Nothing seemed to suggest that this bright, energetic woman's future would not be promising, but that all changed when, on March 2, 1998, Suzanne Lyall stepped off a city bus and has not been seen since.

On Sunday, March 1, 1998, Suzanne called her mother to express her regrets at not being able to celebrate her mother's birthday that evening with family and friends. She had two important tests the next day. Her family understood. She was a serious student, excited about what she was learning. They knew she'd be home for spring break soon and would spend plenty of time with her. They passed the phone around and Suzy happily chatted with everyone at the celebration.

March 2, 1998, started out as a regular day for Suzanne Lyall. She attended all of her classes. She reported for work at 5 o'clock at Babbages, a software store in the Crossgates Mall. Nothing seemed out of the ordinary. At 7:30 that evening, she visited the store Mrs. Field's in the mall and bought a snack of a cookies After work, Suzanne caught the 9:20 bus for her ride back to campus.

Back at campus, at 9:45, on Collins Circle, a dormmate was getting on another bus and saw Suzanne get off her bus. She was not a friend of Suzanne's; she had just seen Suzanne around campus and the dorm, so she did not speak with her. However, she distinctly remembers her hair and coat as she exited the bus. That is the last known sighting of Suzanne Lyall. She disappeared on her two hundred-yard walk back to her dorm room.

The next morning, Richard Condon, Suzanne's boyfriend, called the Lyalls to report that he could not locate Suzanne. She and Richard had met online three years earlier. The Lyalls knew immediately something was wrong. Suzanne was in the habit of e-mailing her parents nightly and they had not received an e-mail from their daughter the night before. They called the university police who went to check on her and

reported back to her parents that Suzanne was not in her room. Suzanne did not show up for her 11:15 a.m. class. A search effort was mobilized immediately for the missing girl.

On March 3rd, at 3:56 p.m., the ATM at a local Stewart's Convenience Store was accessed using Suzanne's card. The card company confirmed that the PIN number used was punched correctly the first time. The user withdrew $20, even though the account had one hundred dollars available for withdrawal. At first, this raised hopes. Suzanne, a typical college student, rarely withdrew or carried with her more than $20. Could Suzanne still be in the area? Maybe she had become ill and was confused. The police requested the videotape from the surveillance camera at the store.

Unfortunately, the cameras were not focused on the customers; rather, they were pointed at the cashier to prevent theft. Because of diligent police work, the police were able to identify and interview all of the customers, except one, who checked-out at the Stewarts in the half hour before and the half hour after Suzanne's ATM card was used. None of them reported seeing a woman matching Suzanne's description. Police are still looking for the last man who has not yet been identified. He is not considered a suspect but police would like to question him. He is described as an African-American male, wearing a Carhartt style work jacket and a black Nike baseball cap. He has become known as the "Nike man."

Who had used Suzanne's card? Was it her abductor? If it was an abductor who had forced Suzanne's PIN number from her, why hadn't he taken all her money? Was it someone who knew Suzanne's PIN number? Only Suzanne and her boyfriend knew her PIN number. Something was terribly wrong.

An artist's sketch of the "Nike Man."
Courtesy of the Doe Network.

Questions plagued investigators. Had Suzanne Lyall gotten on the bus at Crossgates Mall after work? While a driver thought she had gotten on the bus, he couldn't be exactly sure of the date. She traveled on the bus often. Could someone have offered Suzanne a ride at her job or perhaps abducted her there? Had she really gotten off the bus at her dorm? The person who saw her did not personally know Suzanne; she had just seen her around the dorm and campus, and maybe she was confused about the night in question, after all, like the bus driver, Suzanne took the bus often and got off at this stop regularly. If she made it back to campus on the bus as witnesses claim, perhaps someone was in the parking lot waiting for her.

Two months after her disappearance, a weather-worn, out-dated work identification card of Suzanne's was found in the back of the parking lot she would have passed on her way to the dorm. To make matters worse, a source close to Suzanne falsely reported seeing Suzanne in an entirely different part of New York, wasting police efforts chasing false leads. While the Lyalls have their suspicion, to date, not one credible shred of evidence has surfaced to the whereabouts of Suzanne Lyall. Where is Suzanne?

MISSING

Audrey Herron.
Courtesy of Jeanne and Ray Turk.

HAVE YOU SEEN THIS WOMAN?

Audrey Herron

Race: White
Sex: Female
DOB: October 4, 1970
Height: 5'0"
Weight: 105 lbs.
Eyes: Hazel
Hair: Light Brown
Last Seen: Leaving Columbia Green Long-Term Health Facility at approximately 11:10 p.m. on August 29, 2002, in her 1994 black Jeep Grand Cherokee, license plate X233UV. Neither Audrey nor her car has ever been located. If you know anything about Audrey Herron, please contact the New York State Police at 518-622-8600.

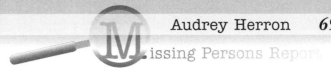

Audrey Herron

In one of her pictures, Audrey Herron is facing forward, but her eyes look sideways as if she didn't want to stay still for the picture. It is as if she is ready to run off on another adventure. Her lips are spread in a wide impish grin. Audrey was a little spitball of fire, just thirty-one years old at the time of her disappearance; she stood barely five feet tall and had a slight frame. She had thick, beautiful light brown hair with blonde highlights. She had big hazel eyes and a friendly grin. Audrey was a beautiful woman inside and out.

Audrey worked per diem at Columbia Green Long Term Health Facility. Her patients remember her as a compassionate caregiver. Her family and friends remember her as energetic and spontaneous. She had great sense of humor and was naturally upbeat. She considered herself a "Nineties Woman," modern, independent, and spunky. She rode a motorcycle and loved going to the mall. She gave friends fashion advice. She loved to dance and have fun. Just before she disappeared, she was planning a fishing trip with her mother and her good friend, Marie.

She was also a dedicated mother. She had three children. Her first child, Sonsia, was ten at the time of her disappearance. Sonsia was from a previous relationship with a man named Dave Court; Dave had wanted to marry Audrey, but she had other plans in mind. Sonsia was active in Brownie Girl Scouts and Audrey always volunteered countless hours to help make her daughter's and other young girls' experience rewarding. Her friends recall Audrey always receiving awards for her work with the Girl Scouts.

Audrey was married to Jeffrey Herron, and had been for about five years before her disappearance. Jeff worked with his parents at the golf course. Audrey and Jeff had two children, Quinn, only one years old at the time of Audrey's disappearance, and Katie, who was four. Audrey loved being a mother. Everyone said it was what she lived for.

Audrey worked per diem, therefore her schedule changed from week to week. She loved helping people and her welcoming smile and compassionate manner were a great aid to many families when their loved ones were sick. On August 29, 2002, Audrey was working the second shift. She called her husband around 9 p.m. to give him the good news that she had just gotten a raise she had been hoping for. At 11 p.m., when her shift ended, she walked with some co-workers out to the parking lot. They chatted for a short while and then Audrey climbed into her 1994 black, Jeep Grand Cherokee, with a New York license plate X233UV. Her co-workers watched her pull out of the lot onto State Route 23 headed westbound. That is the last time anyone has seen Audrey Herron.

Jeffrey Herron claimed he woke up sometime after midnight and noticed that Audrey was not at home. At 2:30 a.m. Jeff Herron placed a phone call to his own father. He claimed it was to tell his father that Audrey was not at home. Jeff did not call the healthcare facility until 6 a.m. the next morning to ask about the whereabouts of his wife. He had assumed she had been asked to work a second shift and was surprised to find out she had not. Around 9:30 the next morning, Jeffery Herron called Ray and Jeanne Turk, Audrey's parents, to ask if they knew where Audrey was. Ray knew right away something was wrong. He called the police and the search began.

The police leapt into action looking for Audrey. Helicopters climbed into the air. Searchers on foot began walking the route Audrey would have taken on her twelve-mile drive home. Not only was Audrey missing, but also was her 1994 black Jeep Cherokee. An intensive search turned up absolutely no evidence. Audrey's husband made a tearful plea for Audrey to return, suggesting to investigators and the media

that Audrey may have left on her own because of an argument they had. In the ensuring days, Audrey's ex-boyfriend, Dave Court, was asked to take a lie detector test. He took it and passed. His daughter, Sonsia, moved back with her dad. Jeff Herron was asked to take a lie detector test. He initially agreed, but the test was never completed. Herron's father interrupted the test with a request that Jeff consult a lawyer before completing the test.

On October 8, 2004, a posting was made to an Internet website. The poster claimed to be Audrey Herron. In the post, the author claimed that Audrey was fine and living in Florida. Hopes soared that Audrey had finally been found. However, police investigators found the posting to be a cruel hoax by a Canadian teenager. More false hope was raised when a trucker claimed he had given a ride to Audrey. This also turned out to be a false lead. Police tirelessly and doggedly followed each and every lead and they all led to the same place — nowhere.

Family, friends, and investigators believe that someone knows what happened to Audrey and her vehicle. Was someone hiding in her car as she left the hospital? Did someone stage an accident and abduct Audrey? Did Audrey make it home that evening? Was someone waiting for her in her driveway? Where is Audrey?

MISSING

Brian Sullivan.
*Courtesy of Barbara
and Daniel Sullivan.*

HAVE YOU SEEN THIS MAN?
Brian Sullivan

Race: White
Sex: Male
DOB: December 5, 1987
Height: 5'11"
Weight: 170 lbs
Eyes: Brown
Hair: Brown
Last Seen: July 8, 2007, 5:48 a.m. Burger King, Chili Avenue, Gates, New
York. That same morning, at 6:10 a.m., he left a voice mail message on a
friend's phone.
Circumstances of Disappearance: Brian's red, 1995 Pontiac Sunbird was found
on Lettington Avenue, Gates, New York. If know anything about Brian
Sullivan, please contact the Monroe County Sheriff at 585-753-4177.

Brian Sullivan

When you visit the Sullivans' home, the first thing you notice on their front steps is a large pair of white sneakers. They are Brian's...awaiting his return. Brian was a tall, handsome, young man on the brink of adulthood when he disappeared. He was a graduate of Churchville-Chili High School and had attended Monroe Community College. He loved Rap music and wrote songs prolifically — he had hoped one day to make a mark in the music world with his creative lyrics and innovative beats. He also loved nature and sometimes would sit outside, under the trees, to get inspiration for his writing. Brian loved meeting people and loved being out and about. He was not a homebody. He had a wide grin and an open heart.

However, like most young people, Brian was restless, too. He was feeling the calling of bigger things, yet not quite sure how to pursue his dreams. His parents, hoping to prod him into a direction, told him he had a week to decide where his immediate future was going: school, job, or a place of his own. The deadline of his decision was upon them. What would Brian choose? Brian was talking about going back to school, getting his degree, getting the skills he needed before he moved on in life...and then he was gone.

July 7, 2007, was a typical day. Brian had on blue shorts, flip-flops, a button-down shirt, and a green baseball cap to control his long curly hair. It was going to be a night of hanging out with his friends, watching a movie, something to do on a hot summer night. Brian, like many young men his age, was a night owl.

With the sun on the rise, Brian decided to go through the drive-thru at the local Burger King for breakfast. He was last seen in the drive-thru at the Chili Avenue Burger King at 5:38 a.m. At 6:10, he called a good friend and left a message on his voice mail. That is the last time anyone has ever heard from Brian Sullivan. His 1995, red Pontiac Sunfire was found at the end of Lettington Avenue, in front of the woods. The remains of his Burger King breakfast in the backseat, along with his wallet.

No one realized right away that Brian was missing. His family knew he had been out with friends, thinking about his future. They knew he liked to stay out late, but it was odd for him not to come home or call. Everyone was getting on with their day. Brian would want a change of clothes, a chat with his parents, he'd be home any minute. Early afternoon, the police called the Sullivans to report Brian's car parked in front of a heavily wooded area on Lettington Avenue. His parents drove over. Everything seemed to be in order in the car, but where was Brian? This was an odd spot to leave his car. It was at the end of a road, on a cul-de-sac, near a heavily wooded area. Had Brian gone to visit someone in a friend's car and left his car here? Had he decided to go for a walk in the woods? His parents decided to leave it there for the time being, believing Brian would be back. However, there was a growing concern. Brian would not go anywhere without his wallet and it was still in the car. While his phone charger was in the car, his cell phone was missing.

Later that day, Brian had not returned to his car. His parents knew in their hearts something was seriously wrong. Leaving his car and not getting in touch with family or friends was out-of-character for Brian. If Brian did decide to leave the area, he definitely would have taken his car and his ATM card. Maybe Brian had gone for a walk in the woods and become lost or injured. After all, he loved nature and it would not be uncommon for him to go off into the woods to think or work on his lyrics. A search was conducted and turned up nothing.

M issing Persons Report

His parents initially believed that Brian would just walk through the door. Days turned to weeks, weeks to months, and then months to years. The family showered the area with posters, pounded the pavement, even erected a billboard with Brian's picture and missing information. They hired psychics and a private investigator who took their money, but gave them no leads. No one had heard from or seen Brian since the night he went missing.

If he has been the victim of foul play, where is the evidence? Why would he park at the end of a cul-de-sac in the early morning hours? Did someone lead Brian to that spot and then kidnap him? Did they abduct him first and then abandon the car at the end of the road? Did Brian become injured while out in the woods and wander off? Was he just tired of small town life in upstate New York and take off? If so, why didn't he take his car with him? There are many more questions than answers. Brian has not used his cell phone or accessed his bank account since his disappearance. Where is Brian?

Brian Sullivan with short hair. *Courtesy of Barbara and Daniel Sullivan.*

MISSING

Sharon Shechter.
Courtesy of Sandra Poole.

HAVE YOU SEEN THIS WOMAN?
Sharon Shechter

Race: White
Sex: Female
DOB: February 10, 1966
Height: 5'4"
Weight: 145 lbs
Eyes: Brown
Hair: Brown
Last Seen: December 9, 2001 leaving her home on Nettle Creek Road, Perinton, to pick up her children from a weekend with their father around 5 p.m.
Circumstances of Disappearance: Sharon was scheduled to pick up her children from her estranged husband at 5:30 p.m. on December 9, 2001. According to her husband, she called and asked him to keep the children and bring them to school the next day. On December 12, 2001, her van was found at the Days Inn Hotel, Chili Avenue, Gates, with Sharon's blood inside. If you know anything about Sharon Shechter, please contact the Monroe County Sheriff at 585-753-4177.

Sharon Shechter

Sharon Shechter of Perinton, New York, was a vibrant woman whose life revolved around her small children, ages 5, 7, and 9. She was a petite, pretty, active woman. She was a loving and devoted mother and a kind, caring friend. She and her mother, Sandra Poole, were very close and spoke on the phone two to three times a day. Her life had not been easy in the days before her disappearance. The former teen beauty queen was in the process of a divorce from her husband, Alan, a man whom she had a restraining order against. Times were tough, but it was almost Christmas and nothing could quash her vivacious, upbeat spirit. After all, her kids had adjusted to the separation and her life was finally looking up.

On Sunday, December 9, 2001, Sharon's children were with her husband for the weekend. She decided to use the weekend to get some Christmas shopping done while her children were away. She talked with her mother at noon on that day by phone, telling her of her plans for the day; lunch with her friend, Mike, shopping, and then picking up the children at 5:30 p.m. Shortly after talking with her mother, she and Mike had lunch at a nearby restaurant and went shopping together. Mike dropped her off at the house around 5 p.m.

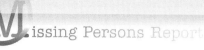

Shortly after Mike drove away, neighbors saw Sharon as she turned on the outdoor Christmas lights. Always thinking about her children, she had wanted the lights to be on when the children got home. A little while later, neighbors reported seeing Sharon's 1992 Maroon Dodge Caravan leaving the driveway; they assumed she was on her way to pick up her children.

Sandy Poole tried calling her daughter that evening. No one picked up the phone. Sandy assumed Sharon was busy with the kids and wasn't overly concerned, but she did think it was a little odd. Sharon usually took her mother's calls. Sharon did not report for work the next morning and her co-workers called the police. The police went over to the home and found nothing out of the ordinary. Sharon's mother went over to her daughter's home. The alarm system was activated and nothing was out of the ordinary. Homemade Christmas ornaments were still on the table where Sharon had been working on them. Sharon's husband indicated that Sharon had called him between 5 and 5:30 and asked him to keep the children because she had something to do that evening. She told her husband to take the children to school in the morning. Something did not sound right. That was not like Sharon and her mother contacted the police who came and searched the home. Calls were made to all her friends. No sign of Sharon could be found anywhere, and her van was also missing.

On Wednesday, December 12, 2001, Sharon's van was found in the parking lot of the Days Inn in Gates, New York. Inside were bloodstains identified as Sharon's. However, no other evidence as to what happened to Sharon could be found in the van.

She had not registered as a guest at the hotel and no one recalled seeing a woman who fit Sharon's description in the area. Had someone abducted Sharon? Was she a victim of foul play? Witnesses did report seeing a Jamaican man with the van the day before. Does this man know something about Sharon's disappearance?

No one has seen or heard from Sharon since her disappearance. Sharon's mother has her own ideas about what happened to her daughter. She knows her daughter would never have willingly left her children behind, but right now, all she has is theories and hope. Where is Sharon?

MISSING

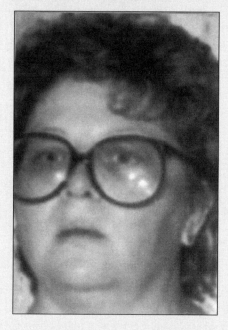

Judith Guerin.
Courtesy of Amy Kusaywa.

HAVE YOU SEEN THIS WOMAN?

Judith A. Guerin

Race: White
Sex: Female
DOB: October 6, 1945
Height: 5'3"
Weight: 180 lbs
Eyes: Hazel
Hair: Blonde
Last Seen: January 28, 1991, at the Rondeen Trailer Park, Margaretta Road,
Sodus Point, New York. If you know anything about Judith Guerin, please
contact the Wayne County Sheriff at 315-946-9771.

Judith A. Guerin

Grief makes people behave in ways that can't be predicted. Judith Guerin was a mother of three children, a girl and two boys, when her husband, Joseph, passed away suddenly of a heart attack in 1988. He was only fifty-seven years old. Up until that moment her life had been perfect; raising her kids and being a stay at home mom while her husband worked as an Albany County Sheriff. Life was happy in the comfortable four-bedroom home.

Joseph left behind a generous life insurance and a pension from the Sheriff's office, but it takes more than money to get a family through the loss of a loved one. Judith, who was a teetotaler before her husband's death, turned to alcohol to dull the pain she felt. Everyone noticed the change in her. She started to spend her evenings out drinking and less and less time with her family. Her children were hurt and confused, hoping that their mother would "snap out of it." In 1989, Judith sold the family home and bought a duplex. It wasn't until moving day that the children found out their mother did not plan to move in with them. Judith had plans to move in with a younger man, Curtis Pucci, she had met out while drinking. Amy, Judith's oldest, became her younger brothers' guardian. Amy was confused and angry. How could their mother do this? Still, she hoped with time, their mother would come to her senses and return to the family.

Judith and her new boyfriend moved to Sodus Point, a small community on Lake Ontario outside of Rochester, New York. The money from Joseph's

life insurance was dwindling fast. Judith and her boyfriend, Curtis, lived in a small trailer. Finally, as the money started to give out, Judith, who hadn't worked before, was forced to find work at a nearby motel-restaurant. Judith and Curtis continued to drink heavily. Her co-workers reported that Judith had started to show up at work with bruises. Even though her life was continuing to spiral downwards, she always called her children once a week to see how they were doing.

Judith reached the bottom when she was arrested for writing two bad checks and later for DWI. She told her daughter how stupid she felt for getting herself in such trouble. Amy told her mother to come home. Together, they would get her help and start life anew. Amy was very hopeful this time that her mother was finally coming to her senses and would soon be home with her family. That was the last time Amy spoke with her mother.

A few weeks went by before Amy began to grow concerned. The Christmas holidays had passed and she hadn't heard from her mother. It was unlike her mother, even with her troubled life, to go for such a long period without contacting her children. Amy called her mother's work and found she had stopped showing up. She contacted Curtis Pucci, who indicated that he believed Judith had taken off for Florida. Amy did not believe her mother would go to Florida and not let her children know. Amy then contacted the local police. They told Amy her mother had most likely left on her own to escape an abusive relationship and prosecution on the charges she was facing.

Amy started to make trips to Sodus Point to find out any information on her mother. Shortly after Judith's disappearance, Pucci began to sell Judith's personal items such as jewelry. If Judith had fled to Florida, like Pucci claimed, why hadn't she taken her jewelry? Pucci eventually sold the trailer they lived in and moved. As witnesses talked to Amy about her mother's relationship with Pucci, the depth of the abuse her mother had suffered under Pucci began to emerge. Maybe her mother had fled suddenly to get away from this man, but if she had, why didn't she

come home or at least tell her children where she was going? Again and again, as Amy asked people where they thought her mother was, Amy most often heard the reply, "In the lake."

Still the police refused to listen to Amy. They insisted that her mother had left on her own accord. There was no proof of a crime. People do that when they get into trouble, the police claimed, they disappear. Amy understood that her mother was in legal trouble, but since she was a first-time offender, she would not be facing jail time. Amy couldn't believe she would flee to avoid prosecution, but no one would listen to her. If Judith left on her own, Amy believed that a paper trail would lead to her. Her mother never accessed any of her money, claimed any benefits, or filed a tax return. Something was terribly wrong. As much as Judith had her problems, she never would have totally abandon all contact with her children. Even though no one would listen to Amy and her mother's trail was going cold, Amy refused to give up looking for her mother.

The search wore heavily on Amy. The trip to Sodus Point was a 400-mile-round trip. Still she persisted. Amy never thought that it would take years, but it did. Year after year, Amy contacted the local police and year after year she was told the same thing — there was no evidence of a crime. Amy finally married a Sheriff officer, like her dad, and he was able to help her in the search. Thirteen years after Judith Guerin went missing, the police took their first missing person's report from Amy. It was a bittersweet victory for Amy, though, as the trail had gone cold long before this.

Did Judith Guerin leave to flee an abusive relationship or out of fear of prosecution for her bounced checks and DWI? Amy doesn't believe so. If she did flee, why didn't she contact her children and let them know she was safe? Why didn't she claim benefits, such as social security or draw on her husband's pension? Was she a victim of foul play? Kidnapping? Does Curtis Pucci know more than he is telling? Where is Judith?

issing Persons Report

MISSING

Jaliek Rainwalker.
Courtesy of Barbara Reeley.

HAVE YOU SEEN THIS MAN?
Jaliek Rainwalker

Race: Mixed race, White and Black
Sex: Male
DOB: November 2, 1995
Height: 5'6"
Weight: 105 lbs
Eyes: green
Hair: Brown
Last Seen: November 1, 2007, at the Red Robin Restaurant, Latham, New York with his father, Stephen Kerr.
Circumstances of Disappearance: Kerr claims Jaliek ran away sometime during the night of November 1, 2007, or the early hours of November 2, 2008. If you know anything about Jaliek Rainwalker, please contact the Greenwich Village Police at 518-692-9332.

Jaliek Rainwalker

We'd like to believe that all children come into the world loved and provided for. We want to believe that infants will be protected from the harshness of life until they are old enough mentally and emotionally to understand that life is not always a safe place. Unfortunately, we know this is not always the case. Too many children are born into situations that are deeply complex and disturbing. When a pregnant woman abuses drugs, her child is born addicted and has to spend the first few days of his fragile life facing a difficult withdrawal. However, the problems do not end when the drugs are safely out of the baby's system. These addicted newborns face a lifetime of physical, mental, and emotional difficulties. This was the situation Jaliek Rainwalker was born into on November 2, 1995.

Jaliek was born to a prostitute at home. The drug-addicted mother didn't know who had fathered Jaliek and, even if she suspected, the chances of knowing the man's name were miniscule. When Jaliek was two days old, his mother took him to a local emergency room, where a blood test showed cocaine in the baby's system. Child Protective Services removed Jaliek from his birth mother's care.

Jaliek spent five years in foster care, bouncing from home to home, living in seven placements in the first five years of his life. Like other children born addicted, he needed therapy. Jaliek lacked fine motor skills, which required regular occupational and physical therapy. He also had speech difficulties and saw a speech therapist. However, his behavioral and

mental health problems were more difficult to treat. He was diagnosed with reactive detachment disorder, a disorder that arises from improper bonding at birth. A foster mother of Jaliek's remembers him climbing into the laps of total strangers and crying inconsolably when taken away. Children with this disorder have difficulties forming normal, healthy relationship bonds. Jaliek also had difficulties controlling his anger and was prone to tantrums.

Despite his difficulties, many people described Jaliek as a warm, loving, caring boy who never complained and was making headway in overcoming his difficulties. His grandmother, Barbara Reeley, describes him as kind and gentle to animals and helpful with his younger sister, also adopted. It seemed the worst of Jaliek's problems were over when he came into the foster care of Stephen Kerr and Jocelyn MacDonald.

Kerr and MacDonald had none of their own natural children. They had wanted a big family, so they opened their home as foster parents to Jaliek and another child. Eventually, Kerr and MacDonald adopted both their foster charges. Kerr and MacDonald received about $1,500 per adoptive child to help provide for their extra care. Jaliek saw his therapists regularly. He continued to make headway and improve. His future was starting to look bright, no longer determined by the difficult circumstances of his birth. However, after Jaliek and his sister's adoption was finalized, things changed rapidly for the family.

Kerr and MacDonald moved the family from their beautiful Victorian home into a rustic, two-room house with no electricity, central heating, or running water. They had wanted to return to a simpler way of living. They raised chickens and goats. Jaliek and his siblings were taken out of public school and home-schooled. Jaliek stopped seeing his therapists. Though Jaliek didn't necessarily like the new living arrangements, he adapted as best he could.

Over time, his adoptive parents claimed he was volatile and the other children were afraid of Jaliek. They decided they could no longer care for Jaliek and were planning on disrupting the adoption and sending Jaliek back to foster care. Whether Jaliek knew of their plans is unclear. The final straw came when Jaliek made an inappropriate remark to another child in his home-school group. The child, a four-year-old, was picking at Jaliek's shoelaces to annoy him. Jaliek asked the youngster to stop several times, but when he continued to harass Jaliek, Jaliek said, "Stop, or I will stick my dick up your butt." The home-school group teacher, while recognizing the comment was inappropriate, did not think Jaliek truly meant any harm. He was just a pre-teen being a pre-teen. He did not act overtly angry or upset. However, Jaliek's mother, Jocelyn, was horrified by the comment and said that Jaliek was no longer welcomed in their house with the other children. Since Jaliek's mother and father were temporarily separated, Jaliek's father was given full care of Jaliek while his mother took the other children to town to live with relatives.

Jaliek's father was called away on family business and asked a former foster family of Jaliek's if the boy could spend the week. Foster respite care is common. It gives both the family and the child a cooling off period so both sides can decide how to precede in a safe and healthy way. The Persons, the foster care family, readily agreed and Jaliek's father dropped him off at their house. Jaliek was given his school assignments and an added assignment from his father: he was to write an apology letter to everyone he had hurt.

By all accounts, Jaliek spent a happy week with the Persons. No one noticed anything out of the ordinary. He did his homework and wrote the apology letters. He also participated in family activities and, while he would be at home with his father for the weekend, he was looking forward to spending a second week with the Persons.

Stephen Kerr arrived to pick up Jaliek on November 1, 2007. Things seemed tense between the two. Stephen was not pleased to find that his son had really enjoyed the week in the Persons' care. Stephen took Jaliek out for dinner that evening. The waitress who served the two reported that Jaliek and

his father did not speak. Kerr had ordered Jaliek's meal for him. Besides his father, that is the last time anyone has seen or heard from Jaliek.

Jaliek's father says they rented a movie and went home to watch it. After the movie, he and Jaliek went to bed. When he awoke, Kerr said, Jaliek was gone. Kerr called the police at 8:57 a.m. to report Jaliek missing. Kerr believed the boy had runaway. A massive search of the area was performed, but no sign of Jaliek was found.

From the beginning there were inconsistencies with Stephen Kerr's story. Based on cell tower records, Kerr did not take the route home from Latham to Greenwich he claimed to have taken the night he and Jaliek had dinner. Kerr claims he did not leave home that evening, but there is evidence suggesting otherwise. Kerr declined a polygraph test. The day Jaliek went missing he attended a work-sponsored outing and only mentioned his son missing in passing. Jaliek's family continued to maintain that Jaliek had left on his own. Jaliek's grandmother, Barbara Reeley, was not as convinced and has mounted a massive search for her grandson.

On February 2, 2008, a note was received at several area newspapers and television stations. It had a Westchester County postmark, over two hundred miles away. The note read: "*Jaliek still alive. Needed a foot soldier for this war on drugs. Picked him up Rt 40 Post 30. He's ok. No fake. He says asks his Mama and Papa/ Who are the macaronni (sic) family? My cat name diamond? Why does Franti yell fire? Don't try to look we are not there.*" The information in the note suggested that if the note was not written by Jaliek, it was written by someone who knew Jaliek or his family. People close to Jaliek believe the note was a prank.

What happened to Jaliek? To date, not a trace of the boy has been found. His adoptive family moved to Vermont shortly after Jaliek's disappearance. They maintain that Jaliek ranaway. Did he runaway from his adoptive family, as they claim, and now is living somewhere under an assumed identity? Was he abducted? Or was he the victim of something much more sinister. Where is Jaliek?

Part Three

The Unidentified

E ach year, police agencies around the nation find human remains
that cannot be identified. While the police collect all the evidence
in the location the body is found, in the case of the unidentified
missing, none of this information leads to an identification. Sometimes
police find only partial or severely decomposed remains and there is no
usable evidence. Police will collect DNA, fingerprints, and other evidence
to help identify the victim; however, even if DNA and fingerprints are
available, if the unidentified does not have DNA or fingerprints on record
no match can be made.

   The FBI's National Crime Information Center (NCIC) keeps record
on all unidentified people — dead and alive — reported to the FBI.
The NCIC categorizes the missing unidentified as deceased, victims of
catastrophe, or living persons whose identification cannot be determined
(babies, amnesia, dementia suffers, etc.) As of December 31, 2009, the
NCIC reported 7,302 unidentified persons. It is important to note,
however, just like missing people, there is no law that requires agencies
to report unidentified remains to the FBI. This can hinder returning
the remains of loved ones home to their family for proper burial and
memorials. Every single unidentified person is a missing person and
someone is looking for him or her. Many, though not all, unidentified
people have died as the result of a crime. Identifying victims can help
police bring criminals to justice.

The information in this section is about unidentified remains found in New York State. It is quite possible that many of these unidentified remains are not New Yorkers, but by getting information out there about these people, maybe we can jog someone's memory. All the pictures in this section were provided by the Doe Network (see listing in the "Source Book" section), a national volunteer organization that helps police agencies find missing people. The pictures accompanying the unidentified stories were created by forensic artists. These artists used the human remains and their skills in drawing, digitally enhanced photography, or sculpture to create life-like images to help jog people's memories. These photographs are only a suggestion of what the unidentified person may have looked like. If you think you recognize any of them or anything about their story sounds familiar, please do not hesitate to contact the police agency listed or the Doe Network. Remember, someone is waiting, and has been waiting a very long time, to know what has happened to their loved one.

John Does: Unidentified Male Remains

Author's Note: All of the images in this section were provided by the Doe Network.

John Doe – White Infant

Date Discovered: February 27, 1987

This is the sweater Baby Doe was found wrapped in on February 27, 1987.

This newborn baby boy was discovered by the guardrail on the south side of Walworth-Marion Road in Marion. His date of birth was estimated between February 25 to 27, 1987, and therefore thought to be a day or two old. He was 19-1/2 inches long and weighed 6-1/2 pounds. He was born alive. He has brown hair and brown eyes. He was wrapped in the adult sweater pictured above. If you have any information about this baby, contact the New York State Police at 585-398-4100.

John Doe – White Male

Date Discovered: November 8, 1990

Artist's likeness of the remains a hiker found in Bear Mountain State Park on November 8, 1990.

Bear Mountain State Park is a popular hiking area because of its proximity to the New York City metropolitan area. This man was located in the park near where the Appalachian Trail (a trail that runs from Georgia to Maine) crosses the park. He was approximately 45-60 years old, between 5'8" and 6' and had a medium build. He was carrying a Bronkaid Mist inhaler, which asthmatics use to help with their breathing.

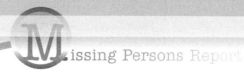

He was wearing Andre Franxois jeans, a t-shirt, and Hi-Tec hiking boots, size 11-1/2. He was wearing a gold chain, carrying a money clip with the logo Klein Tools, and a pocket knife. He was also carrying a wallet, but it had nothing in it to identify him. He was wearing a knapsack with a tag that read "RJ Bass, 2102 Kentucky, Washington DC." This address has not aided in identifying him. He was also carrying a compass, a book of matches from the Bear Mountain Inn, and the novel *Notebooks of Malte Laurids Brigge* by Rainer Maria Rilke. If you have any information about this hiker, please contact the New York State Police at 845-786-2781.

John Doe – White Male

Date Discovered: September 14, 1991

Artist's likeness of a man found in a swamp in Slate Hill on September 14, 1991.

Though his remains were discovered in 1991, this man is thought to have died sometime between 1974 and 1981. He was located in a swamp off Eaton Lake, Slate Hill. He was estimated to be 60 to 65 years old and stood 5'8" tall. He was wearing blue pants, a yellow, long-sleeve shirt, a sweater, and blue socks. Found with the man were a pair of gray bifocals with the name of Orange County Optician, D. J. Riehle. The glasses were manufactured by Swank Opticians sometime between 1974 and 1978. He was nearsighted. Other items found with the man was one shoe, size 10 and wing-tipped shoe; six keys; a black plastic memo book cover; several coins; a vinyl gym bag; and a t-shirt. There was a black plastic wallet in the right back pants pocket, but no identification. If you have any information about this man, please call the New York State Police at 914-344-5300.

Wing tip shoe found with the unidentified remains.

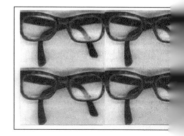

Gray bifocals with the name of Orange County Optician, D. J. Riehle. The glasses were manufactured by Swank Opticians sometime between 1974 and 1978.

issing Persons Report

John Doe – Black Male

Date Discovered: October 9, 1995

Witnesses remember seeing this man on the Metro North train on October 7, 1995, where he traveled to Brewster. His body was located two days later in a wooded area also in Brewster. He is estimated to be between 40 to 50 years old; he stands at 5'9" and weighs 160 pounds. He has black hair with some graying at the temples and has brown eyes. He has a mole on the right side of his nose. If you have any information concerning this case, please contact the New York State Police at 845-279-6161.

Witnesses claim to have seen this man on a Metro North train on October 7, 1995. Two days later his body was found in a wooded area outside of Brewster.

John Doe – White Male

Date Discovered: March 22, 1997

The skeletal remains of this man were discovered by a logger off Harvey Road near the Colonial Hills Apartments in Monticello. He is thought to have died sometime in early 1996 from a self-inflicted gunshot wound to the head. He is estimated to be between 36 to 40 years old and stood at 5'6". Based on his body type and muscle mass, he was well developed and thought to be either a body-builder or a laborer. He was wearing black Levi 550 jeans, a blue hooded sweatshirt, and a black Hanes t-shirt with the words "Puerto Rico" on it and decorated with white palms trees. He wore size 8 Reebok sneakers. He carried a black duffel bag, a yellow flashlight, and a bottle of rum. If you can help identify this man, please call the New York State Police at 845-292-6600.

Likeness of a suicide victim found off Harvey Road in Monticello.

issing Persons Report

John Doe – Male Infant

Date Discovered: September 7, 1997

"Baby Moses'" grave in Albany. His burned remains were found on September 7, 1997 near the statue of Moses in Albany's Washington Park.

The remains of this infant were found near the statue of Moses in Albany's Washington Park. The baby was estimated to be no more than twelve hours old; his umbilical cord was still attached. This put his date of birth no earlier than September 6, 1997. He had been wrapped in a pillow case and someone tried to burn the body; his race is unknown. The local residents named him "Moses" and buried him in Graceland Cemetery. His grave reads: *Moses Washington, Citizen of Albany, Child of God, September 1977.* If you have any information regarding Moses, please contact the Albany Police Department at 518-462-8011.

John Doe – Black Male

Date Discovered: May 3, 1998

The remains of this homicide victim were found wrapped in plastic near the Long Mountain Rest area on Route 6.

The skeletal remains of this man were found wrapped in plastic near the Long Mountain Rest area on Route 6. He is thought to have died from gunshot wounds sometime in 1985. His death is considered a homicide. He is estimated to be between 25 to 35 years old and was between 5'6" to 5'11". His bones indicate he was knock-kneed. He was wearing a black t-shirt with a design of a rainbow leading to a pot of gold, which reads "*Follow Your Dreams*", a blue zippered Sir Jac jacket, size 32 x 32 (blue or black) jeans, blue boxer shorts, and white Pony sneakers. Also found with the body was a hair pick, a French/English dictionary, a metal nail file, and a yellow lighter. If you have any information concerning this case, please contact the New York State Police at 845-782-8311.

Missing Persons Report

John Doe — Asian (Indian) male

Date Discovered: October 9, 1998

Neighbors knew this man as "Prakash". He died from a fall and has never been identified.

Known around the neighborhood as Prakash, this gentleman was found alive but injured on October 9, 1998, in the garage of 170-19 Henley Road in Queens. He lived in the attic of the garage and was climbing a ladder up to his room when he fell, fatally injuring himself. He was then taken to Mary Immaculate Hospital, where he died three days later before his full identity could be ascertained. He is estimated to be between 50 to 60 years old, stood six feet tall, and weighed 178 to 185 pounds. He has brown eyes, black hair, and wore a mustache. He has two moles on the left side of his nose and a two-inch scar on his chest. He had a prominent white wring around his cornea known as arcus senilis. If you have any information about Prakash, contact the New York City Missing Persons Squad at 1-212-694-7781 or the New York County Medical Examiner's Office at 212-447-2770.

John Doe – White or Hispanic Male

Date Discovered: March 9, 2000

This young man was found murdered near a chain-link fence. His remains were in a wooded area, fifty feet off the shoulder of the eastbound lanes of the Northern State Parkway, east of Wolf Hill Road, in the Town of Huntington. He was thought to have been murdered in December 1999 or January 2000. He had been shot in the head.

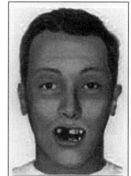

Homicide victim found off the Northern State Parkway.

He is estimated to be 25 to 45 years old, stood 5'8", and weighted between 140 to150 pounds. He had short brown or black hair. He was wearing a khaki colored, short sleeved, v-neck shirt with black trim, a t-shirt from New Jersey depicting a seaside scene with an emblem reading "Atlantic City," size 30 x 32 *Levi L2* blue jeans and a blue bathing suit. He has severely decayed teeth with eight teeth missing. If you have any information about this case, contact the New York State Police at 631-231-6389 or 800-220-TIPS.

John Doe – White or Hispanic Male

Date Discovered: March 26, 2004

This man, a homicide victim, was dead at least 20 years before his body was found on the Northern State Parkway.

The skeletal remains of this man were found in the median, adjacent to a connecting utility road, between east and westbound lanes of Northern State Parkway, between Exits 38 and 39, near Plainview. He is thought to have died at least twenty years before his discovery, which puts his date of death around 1984. He is estimated to be between 23 to 57 years old and was between 4'11" and 5'4". He had a slight build and had a metopic suture, which is a deformity of the skull formed as a child grows. There is also some evidence that he suffered from anemia. He was wearing an expensive Bulova watch with an alligator wrist band. He was wearing tan pleated canvas bell bottom pants with a brown leather cardholder in the pocket. He also had on an orange and blue striped Members Only brand jacket. This jacket was imported to the United States in 1982, which would put his death as early as 1982. His teeth indicate he may have suffered from a prolonged period of fever or illness as a child. If you have any information about this case, contact the New York State Police at 631-756-3300.

John Doe — White
or Hispanic Male

Date Discovered: February 5, 2005

This baby, nicknamed "John Valentine", was found in Rockaway Beach near 112th Street. His body was found in a nautical style canvass bag, wrapped in duct tape, and investigators believe he was tossed into the ocean. However, where the body entered the water is unknown. He could have been thrown from a ship. His head was not found with his remains, making identification more difficult. His death has been ruled a homicide after investigators determined the child had unhealed broken bones. He had died a few weeks before discovery. He is thought to be somewhere between three to five years old, making his birth year sometime between 2000 to 2002, stood three feet tall, and weighed twenty-eight pounds. The baby was wrapped in a Dundee-brand Disney crib sheet decorated with Disney characters and letters of the alphabet. If you have any information on John Valentine, please contact the New York City Police Department at 718-318-4224.

The blanket the remains of the baby nicknamed "John Valentine" was wrapped in before his body was dumped into the water.

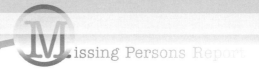

John Doe — White Male

Date Discovered: February 15, 2005

The skeletal remains of this man were found by hikers in the Palisades State Park, three miles off Long Meadow Road in a heavily wooded area in Warwick. He is thought to have died sometime between 1995 and 2000. He was between fifty and fifty-five years old and suffered from a pelvic fracture. Nike sneakers were found with the remains. If you have any information about this case, please contact the New York State Police at 845-782-8311.

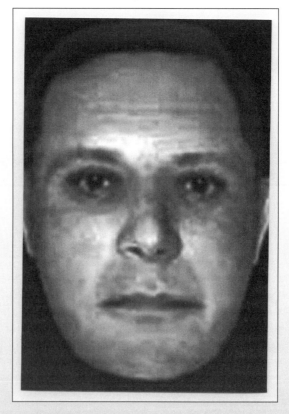

Unidentified hiker found in the Palisades Park.

Jane Does: Unidentified Female Remains

Author's Note: All of the images in this section were provided by the Doe Network.

Jane Doe – White Female

Date Discovered: November 9, 1979

When you look at her photos, it is hard to believe that no one recognizes or misses this sweet-faced girl. "Caledonia Jane," a name given to her by the locals, was found by a passing motorist on the south side of Route 20, a half-mile from the intersection of Route 5 in Caledonia. "Caledonia Jane" was a teenager, her age thought to be somewhere between thirteen and nineteen years old; she's petite, standing only 5'3", and weighing about 120 pounds. She had short, curly, brown hair that had been frosted blonde and pretty brown eyes. A waitress had seen her the evening before in a restaurant in Lima, New York, but could offer no clues as to who she was with or where she was headed. She died of two gunshot wounds: one to her back and one to the front of her head. She had been dead since the evening before her discovery. Investigators determined she was shot by the side of the road, dragged into the cornfield, and shot again.

"Caledonia Jane" is the name given to a young girl found murdered outside of Caledonia.

Several truck drivers came forward to say they saw the girl hitchhiking. She had mentioned she was headed to Boston. Though it was November, she had visible bikini lines, which suggest she had just traveled from a warmer climate. Pollen samples taken from the girl indicated they could only have come from Arizona, California, South Florida, or

Mexico, suggesting she may have recently traveled to or from one of those places. She was wearing a boy's multi-plaid, button-down shirt, tan corduroy pants, blue knee socks, light blue panties, a white bra, brown lace up, ripple-sole shoes, and a red nylon-lined man's windbreaker with black stripes down the arms, marked with the inside label "Auto Sports Products, Inc." She was also wearing a necklace made with silver beads and three small turquoise stones and two key chains that were attached to the front belt loops of her jeans. One key chain, in the shape of a heart, was inscribed, "He who holds the key can open my heart." The other key chain held the key that fit the small silver heart. She was laid to rest in Danville, New York. The grave reads: "Lest we forget an unidentified girl. November 9. 1979. And flights of angels sing thee to thy rest." If you have any information about Caledonia Jane, please call the Livingston County Sheriff's Office at 585-243-7120.

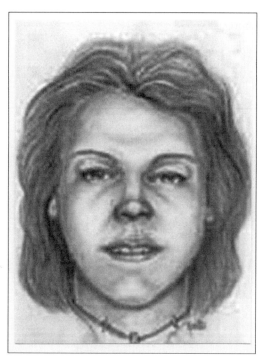

Artist's rendition of "Caledonia Jane."

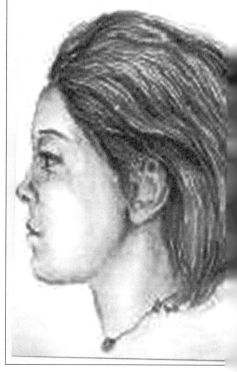

Side view of "Caledonia Jane."

issing Persons Report

Jane Doe – White Female

Date Discovered: December 6, 1983

Artist's drawing of a woman whose remains were found on Route 17 in the town of Ellery. Investigators believe she may have been a foreigner.

This woman, found in a in a ditch along the eastbound lane of Route 17 in the Town of Ellery, is thought to be foreign, possibly from Europe or Canada, based on her dental work, clothing, and items found with the body. She had been shot once in the back, twice in the chest, and once inside the mouth. She is estimated to be between 33 to 37 years old, stood 5'4", and weighed 128 pounds. She had borne at least one child. She had brown hair with a few gray hairs, a wart above her left eye, and a mole behind her left ear. Her blood type was A positive. She has extensive dental work that was most likely performed somewhere in Europe. The clothing she wore was all from Italy: a white V-neck camisole, made in Carpi, and a non-exportable, green, brown, and red checked trench coat, reversible to olive drab wool. She also wore a blue-gray wool crew neck pullover and a handmade plaid wool skirt in shades of brown, blue, and red. She had no shoes and no other personal items with her. The only item found with her remains was a hand-written note from the Blue Boy Motor Lodge in Vancouver, British Columbia. On the note was scribbled some initials and numbers, which the police have not been able to determine their significance. The note read:

- Sar.k.R.h. 24233
- K.R.Ba 68307
- Carg. 74211

She also had an IUD, which was foreign made either in Finland, Belgium, or Holland, and was used in Canada, but not distributed in the USA. If you have any information concerning this case, please contact the Chautauqua County Sheriff's Office at 716-753-4231.

issing Persons Report

Jane Doe – White Female

Date Discovered: July 31, 1988

The complete skeletal remains of this young woman were located in a shallow grave behind 130 Bay Knoll Drive, in Irondequoit, by a young boy digging in his backyard. While the cause of death is undetermined, investigators have ruled her death a homicide. She was believed to have died ten to thirty years before her discovery, which would put her year of death sometime between 1958 to 1978. She is estimated to be between fifteen to twenty years old, but she could be younger. Investigators put her birth year somewhere between 1938 to 1948. She stood between 5'1" to 5'4". She had significant dental restorations using gold foil. If you have any information on this woman, please contact the Monroe County Medical Examiner at 716-274-7970 or the Irondequoit Police Department at 585-336-6000.

The complete skeletal remains of this young woman was found behind a home in Irondequoit. Police believe she was murdered ten to thirty years prior to the discovery of her remains.

Jane Doe – Infant Female, White or Hispanic

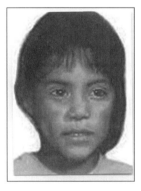

The body of this baby, named "Baby Hope" by investigators, was found stuffed into a cooler in a park off the Henry Hudson Parkway.

Date Discovered: July 23, 1991

Named Baby Hope by investigators working her case, this infant was found in a park bordering the southbound lane of the Henry Hudson Parkway, near the Dyckman Street exit, just north of the George Washington Bridge in the upper Manhattan area. Her death has been ruled a homicide. She was asphyxiated and her body showed evidence of sexual abuse. She was wrapped in a black plastic garbage bag and stuffed in a blue 30-quart Igloo cooler. Police believe she was dumped no earlier than July 18, 1991. A witness claimed to have seen a well-dressed couple, possibly Hispanic, carrying a

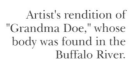

issing Persons Report

picnic cooler fitting the description nine days before Baby Hope's body was found. In October 1991, pornographic Polaroid photos were found on Route 46 in northern New Jersey, near the George Washington Bridge. Police believe these may be photographs of Baby Hope.

Baby Hope was between three and five years old, 3'2" tall, and weighed about thirty pounds. She had long, wavy black hair, held back in a ponytail with a yellow, plastic ponytail holder. She had no clothes, but was found with a light green linen-type cloth. The New York City detectives of the 34th Precinct paid for Baby Hope's burial. She is buried in St. Raymond's Cemetery in the Bronx. If you have any information concerning Baby Hope, please contact the New York City Police Department at 212-927-0823.

Jane Doe – White Female

Date Discovered: September 26, 1995

This woman, nicknamed Grandma Doe by the local police, had only been in the water for a few hours before she was found, leading police to believe she would be quickly identified. However, this has not been the case. Perhaps she went out for a walk, fell into the Buffalo River, near Squaw Island, and accidentally drowned. However, years later, her identity remains a mystery. Grandma Doe is estimated to be between sixty to seventy years old, she had gray hair, was 5'3", and weighed between 150 to160 pounds. She wore a white blouse, light colored slacks, white sneakers, and a light colored (white or cream) trench coat with a butterfly pin. If you have any information about Grandma Doe's case, please contact the Buffalo Police Department at 716-851-4511.

Artist's rendition of "Grandma Doe," whose body was found in the Buffalo River.

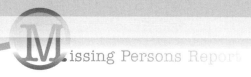

Jane Doe – White Female

Date Discovered: August 15, 2002

Because only her skull was found, police know that identification of this woman will be difficult but not impossible. Thanks to reconstruction, someone may recognize her face. Her skull was found off Platte Clove Road in Hunter. She died somewhere between 1980 and 1990 and was most likely between the ages of twenty-five and fifty-five years old. If you have any information regarding this woman, please contact the New York State Police at 518-622-8600.

An artist reconstruction of a skull found in Hunter with three different hair styles.

Jane Doe – Bi-Racial Female

Date Discovered: August 29, 2002

The skeletal remains of this woman and her seven month fetus were located in a wooded area north of a state fishing access and boat launch to Lake Ontario in the town of Huron. The area where she was found is midway between the cities of Rochester and Syracuse. Her death has been ruled a homicide. Investigators believe she was killed elsewhere and her body dumped in this location. She was wrapped in a tan shower curtain with royal blue shower rings. She may have been a migrant worker who moved in and out of the area. Her date of death is estimated between June and August of 2002. Her age is approximately thirty to forty years old and she stood 5'1" to 5'6" tall. She is thought to be mixed race. If you have any information about this case, please contact the New York State Police at 585-398-4100.

Artist's drawing of a murdered woman, seven months pregnant found at a boat launch on the Town of Huron.

Jane Doe – White Female

Date Discovered: February 10, 2003

Her killer worked hard to make sure she would never be found, but the skeletal remains of this woman were finally discovered in a mostly abandoned apartment building on West 46th Street in New York, in a layer of freshly laid concrete behind an old coal-burning furnace. She had died sometime after 1988.

Artist's drawing of a woman whose remains were found encased in concrete inside an abandoned apartment building in New York City.

She was between fifteen and twenty-one years old and stood 5'2". She had light hair, possibly with a reddish hue. She was wearing a size 32-A bra. She also was wearing a gold-colored ring inscribed with the initials *P Mc G* and a 1966 Bulova watch. If you have any information about this case, please contact the New York City Police 212-473-2042.

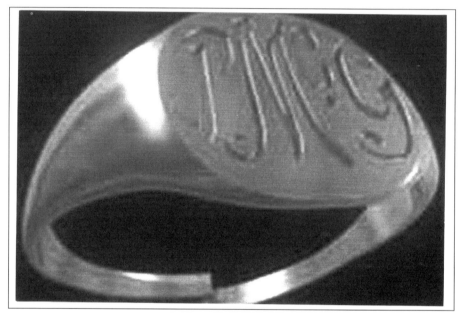

Gold ring woman was found wearing. The initials read P MC G in script.

Jane Doe – Infant Female

Date Discovered: April 5, 2006

This baby, named April Hope by the local police, was found in Mount Kisco. Investigators believe her body was accidentally vacuumed into a truck used to extract sediment and water from catch basins and storm drains throughout neighborhoods in the village of Mount Kisco. Therefore, the exact location that her body was

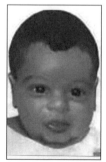

Artist's rendition of a baby named "April Hope" by investigators found in the Village of Mount Kisco.

Missing Persons Report

abandoned is unknown. The community was so moved at the death of this baby that they held a funeral service at the Lutheran Church of the Resurrection and buried her at Oakwood Cemetery. She had dark brown hair, brown eyes, and was less than a day old, which puts her date of birth no earlier than April 4, 2006. If you have any information about this case, please contact the Mount Kisco Police Department at 914-666-3855.

Jane Doe – White Female

Date Discovered: October 13, 2007

Investigators believe this woman was out walking in the Breakneck Mountain, Hudson Highlands State Park, where she was found. She is thought to have died the day before her body was found, October 12, 2007. She is estimated to be between fifty and sixty years old, is 5'5" to 5'8", and weighs 125 to 135 pounds. She has brown, shoulder-length hair, a light completion, and healed pierced ears. She had very mild scoliosis. She was wearing blue Cavaricci® jeans, a blue sweatshirt, a black sweater, black Reebok® hightop sneakers, a brown belt, and red sunglasses. She was carrying an umbrella. She also wore a gold-colored Quartz® watch with black band. Also found with her were a small round compass, a small purple LED flashlight, a brown hair clip, three keys, and a small amount of money. If you have any information about this case, please contact the New York State Park Police at 845-786-2781.

Artist's drawing of a woman who is believed to have died while hiking in Hudson Highland's State Park.

Jane Doe – Black female

Date Discovered: March 31, 2008

The skeletal remains of this woman were found buried in a Manhattan nightclub at 277 Church Street during renovations. She is thought to have died twenty years prior to the discovery of her remains, which puts her death somewhere around 1989. She is estimated to have been between twenty-five and thirty-five years old and stood about 5'4". She had a left tenth rib healed fracture and possible nasal and foot phalanx fractures. Also found with the body were a pair of heart-shaped earrings wrapped in bubble gum wrapper. If you have any information about this case, please contact the New York County Medical Examiner's Office at 212-447-2770.

This homicide victim was found buried in the basement of a New York City nightclub.

Part Four

Searching
for the Missing

With advances in technology and forensics and police science, the search for the missing has become more complex. There is no doubt that police forensics has been the single most driving force in identifying remains and finding the missing. This section is a brief introduction to the search technology and techniques available to investigators and the families of the missing.

The Forensics
of the Unidentified

Letting the Missing
Speak for Themselves

Every unidentified deceased person is also a missing person. As difficult as this is to believe, people die and cannot be identified. Many of these people have been victims of violent crimes. By identifying the deceased, not only will it help solve a crime, but it will help bring answers to the families. According to the FBI's National Crime Information Center, as of its last reporting on January 1, 2008, there were 6,954 unidentified persons in the United States. However, this number represents only those unidentified deceased persons reported to the FBI. According to the U.S. Department of Justice's National Missing and Unidentified Person's System, the actual number of unidentified remains is around 40,000. Coroners, medical examiners, and police agencies are not required to report unidentified bodies to the FBI. These Jane, John, and Baby Does are buried in unidentified graves or cremated, forever remaining anonymous. While advocates continue to work for laws to require the reporting of unidentified bodies, there is no single agency that maintains records on all unidentified deceased persons and all missing persons in the United States. As a result, matches between bodies and the missing are never made.

To make matters worse, in many places, coroners and medical examiners are not required to keep records — such as DNA samples, fingerprints, photographs, or x-rays of the unidentified missing — indefinitely. In many places, unidentified remains are cremated rather than buried because cremations are cheaper than burials. Therefore, if the unidentified records are accidentally lost, such as in a fire or flood, there isn't even hope of a disinterment to check against a missing person's report. In New York State, though strongly recommended, DNA, fingerprints, x-rays, and dental x-rays taken prior to the cremation of an unidentified deceased person are not required. This often results in the families of missing persons wondering if the remains of their loved ones passed through a medical examiner's office and are now buried somewhere in an unmarked grave.

While state and federal governments are working to improve the system of reporting the unidentified deceased and matching them with missing persons reports, significantly more work needs to be done in this area. Until records are kept on every single unidentified person and every missing person, and a system of matching is created, people will fall through the cracks, criminals will get away with heinous crimes, and families of the missing will suffer indefinitely. It is not enough for single states to create these systems. It needs to be a nationwide (if not a worldwide) initiative.

Most people believe that forensic science has to do with dead people and the apprehension of killers. This is because many of the crime shows on television usually deal with murder. However, they are mistaken. Forensics comes from the Latin word "forensic," which means "before the forum." If you lived in ancient Rome and you were accused of a crime, you and your accuser would head to the forum to argue your case. Each side would give a speech to support his or her point. The side that gave the best speech determines the outcome. This is why forensics is also used to describe the study of speech and debate. However, it has also come to mean applying scientific methods to the law or to solve crimes — any crime — not just murder. Forensic science uses all sorts of methods to examine evidence and provide clues. Just like the speakers before the forum, forensic science tries to present the best case possible with the evidence they have collected, studied, and interpreted.

All forensic techniques are based on Locard's Exchange Principle. Dr. Edmond Locard lived from 1877 to 1966 in France. He was one of the first forensic scientists to be employed by a police department. He started the first criminal laboratory in Lyons, France. Locard's Exchange Principle, simply put, tells us that whenever two things come in contact — whether it is people, animals, furniture, etc. — an exchange happens. For example, when I pet my dog, some of her hairs will cling to me or, if I open a door, my fingerprints will be left on that doorknob. After the exchange, the evidence that is left behind is called "trace evidence." That is what forensic investigators are looking for: trace evidence. A forensic scientist will process and study the trace evidence and let it tell its story. If police are looking for a missing person, trace evidence can help tell where the person was before he or she went missing. If investigators are looking at unidentified remains, trace evidence can tell investigators how the person died and give clues to his or her identity.

When a person goes missing or when the police find an unidentified victim, investigators may apply all sorts of forensic methods to determine what may have happened. The type of science investigators decide to use is based on many factors. Whether a thorough scientific investigation takes place depends upon the circumstances of the disappearance, if the investigators believe a crime has been committed, and the experience and services available in the investigating agency.

If the police believe a crime has been committed, they will try to locate the crime scene and collect evidence. For example, if a person was abducted, the investigators may try to find the location of the abduction and look for physical evidence, such as shoe prints, fibers, fingerprints, and blood evidence. If police find an unidentified body, they will try to collect as much evidence as available, such as hair samples, blood, fingerprints, and, most importantly, DNA, if available. They will also look for evidence of a crime.

If the police do not believe a crime has been committed, they may not be willing to conduct a full-scale evidence collection. This is why, if family or friends of the missing find anything out of the ordinary — a broken window, missing items, blood (no matter how small the amount) — they should point it out to investigators immediately. If a family member or friends suspect a crime has been committed, he or she should bring it to the investigators' attention immediately. This may persuade investigators to begin the evidence collection process.

Unfortunately, sometimes experience or finances can play a role in whether a forensic investigation happens. If you live in a rural area, the police agency may never have investigated a missing person's case and they may not be willing to start a full-scale investigation because they do not have the experience or the personnel to do one. However, all police agencies can call for added assistance from the New York State Police.

Types of Evidence

Fingerprints

Whenever a person touches a surface, he or she will leave behind fingerprints. Fingerprints are the ridge detail on the skin. Everyone has fingerprints. What is even more amazing is that no one, not even identical twins, has the same fingerprints. Fingerprint experts can match known prints to prints found at a scene and determine if they are a match. A match will confirm that a person was actually at that location. Police may ask for the fingerprints of the missing person's family members. This does not mean the family members are suspects; investigators need these prints to rule out people who belong in an area and determine if there are unidentified fingerprints.

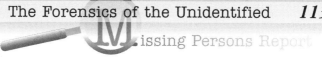

DNA

DNA is short for deoxyribonucleic acid. DNA is hereditary genetic material found in all living things. You get half your DNA from your father and half from your mother. You can think of your DNA as your "blueprint." All human cells contain DNA, which is unique to an individual. The only exception is identical twins. Identical twins are a product of the same egg and sperm that originally started to be one person. However, the fertilized ovum will divide in the first twelve days after fertilization, making two people with the same genetic material. However, identical twins will not have the same fingerprints because fingerprints don't begin to form on a fetus until ten weeks. Therefore, while identical twins have the same genetic material, technically, they are not identical in every way.

Collecting DNA may become very important if the police have evidence that may contain DNA. Again, DNA can be found anywhere that there are human cells: skin, saliva, teeth, hair, etc. The investigators will be able to tell exactly who it came from. They will also be able to match the DNA of the missing person with any unidentified human remains that are found. Investigators will ask for a DNA sample of the missing person, such as a toothbrush or hairbrush. They will then collect DNA samples from both the mother and father, if available. If not, they will collect DNA from the closest family member: a brother, sister, child, aunt, uncle, etc. It is easy and painless to give a DNA sample. The investigator will swab the inside of your cheek with a cotton swab.

However, one of the problems with DNA evidence is it can degrade over time. Some chemicals can also make DNA unusable, which is why sometimes investigators cannot get DNA from skeletal remains.

Other Trace Evidence

Trace evidence refers to any small bits of evidence that is recovered. This evidence can cover just about anything: hair, fibers, clothing, shoe prints, glass, botanical material, and gunshot residue, just to name a few. Investigators remove, preserve, and study these items carefully to determine if there are any clues to the disappearance.

With the advances in technology and forensics, investigators can begin to get clues to help in the search. Police can collect evidence to determine if the person left on their own, was kidnapped, or was a victim of a crime. By gathering, processing, analyzing, and interpreting the evidence, investigators can focus the search and, therefore, have a better chance of locating the missing person. However, it is not easy.

Often times a person is missing for a long period of time before his or her absence is reported. Police may be hesitant to investigate if there is no evidence of a crime, particularly if the investigating agency is small; therefore, losing the chance to collect evidence. There is a current movement in the field of investigation to encourage all law enforcement to treat a missing person investigation the same way that a criminal investigation would be conducted. The last place a person was seen should be investigated fully and so should any other areas that might lead to clues about a person's whereabouts, such as their workplace, car, and home. Amy Kusaywa, the daughter of Judith Guerin, wonders what precious evidence concerning her mother's disappearance was lost forever to time because it took a police agency thirteen years to accept a missing person's report.

Forensic Artists

Forensic artists can help investigators in a variety of ways. Forensic artists can create realistic looking sculptures and pictures to aid in the identification of bodies. They can also "age progress" — that is make a person look older — if that person has been missing for a long time. There are two techniques that are particularly helpful in identifying the deceased and matching them to missing persons. The first is called postmortem reconstruction, which attempts to create a sketch, digital picture, or sculpture of the unidentified person. The second is age progression, which uses existing photographs of a missing person, along with photographs of older family members, to "progress" or age the missing person.

Postmortem Reconstruction

Postmortem Reconstruction is done when the police have recovered an unidentified body and have not been able to identify the deceased by traditional means, such as fingerprints, dental records, or DNA. The forensic artist can work with pictures of a recovered body and information from the medical examiner. However, many times the body has decomposed to the point where there are no recognizable features. Sometimes, the remains are only skeletal and there is no soft tissue left. However, this does not deter the forensic artist from making a three-dimensional reconstruction.

When an unidentified body is discovered intact, the medical examiner may take photographs. The forensic artist can digitally enhance the photographs. Eyes can be opened and eye color added. The artist can add a possible hairstyle and make the photograph look as natural as possible. This photograph can then be used by the investigators and media in an attempt to identify the person. This type of picture is much more helpful than the "morgue" picture. A morgue picture is a picture of the unidentified person taken during the autopsy. Most people cannot identify a person from these types of photographs. The main reason is that it is very disturbing to look at a picture of a dead person and the witness will not examine the picture long enough to identify the person. Many families of the missing are presented with "morgue pictures" in an attempt to identify remains. Family members who have recounted stories of "morgue pictures" found these experiences deeply upsetting, but with a digitally enhanced photograph, witnesses and family members feel more comfortable with the picture because the person looks alive.

When investigators find a decomposed body or skeletal remains, the process takes longer. The reconstruction is done using the skull, or a cast of the skull, and clay. The reconstruction can give investigators an idea what the person might have looked like in life. These sculptures can be photographed and used by investigators and the media to help identify the remains.

The reconstruction artist is a highly trained individual who has a background in art, as well as anatomy and physiology. The artist places markers on the skull to determine tissue depth. Tissue depth is based on anthropological studies of age, sex, race, and body density. After the markers are placed on the skull, the artist places clay over the markers and skull to create a 3-D sculpture. The artist will also add realistic looking eyes and hair. This sculpture is then photographed. While not a perfect representation of the deceased, these sculptures are often close enough to jog witnesses or family members into recognizing the person.

Age Progression

Age progression is an artistic technique where the artist progresses or "moves forward" the age of a person for identification purposes. This technique is used for children and for people who have been missing a long time. Children change very rapidly as they grow, so this useful tool can help investigators by giving them clues as to what a missing person may currently look like. It can also help investigators generate new leads. Artists can use software that digitally progresses a person. However, many artists still hand draw pictures from photographs. The artists will use past pictures of the missing person and pictures of close relatives, such as a parent or sibling, to get an idea of how the missing person would age. They may update the hairstyle and clothing to help jog witnesses' memories.

Kristen Freeborn, Forensic Artist

Kristen Freeborn is a highly trained and gifted freelance forensic artist, living and working in New York State, whose areas of expertise include composite drawing and both 2-D and 3-D forensic facial reconstructions. She works on both current and historical projects. Kristen works with law enforcement and with the families of the missing. She works quickly. From the time Kristen receives the skull to the finished sculpture takes less than two weeks — this can help to get a picture out to the public before precious memories begin to fade further.

All of the following images are courtesy of Forensic Artist Kristen Freeborn.

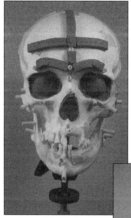

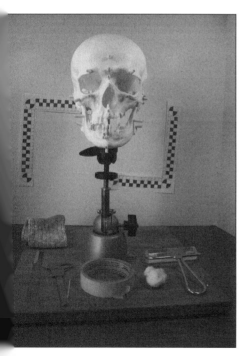

Kristen starts by placing the skull on a secure working stand. She takes careful measurements to help determine the size of the person.

Kristen then begins by placing markers on the skull to determine the depth of the tissue. By examining the skull she can determine if the person may have had any past injuries that would show up as scars on the person's face. After her markers are placed, she starts laying thin strips of clay over the skull to approximate the depth of the tissue and skin, she then carefully smooths the clay to give the face and head shape. She does not use "glass" or colored eyes. In her experience, choosing the wrong eye color could lead a witness to misidentify or not identify the deceased.

issing Persons Report

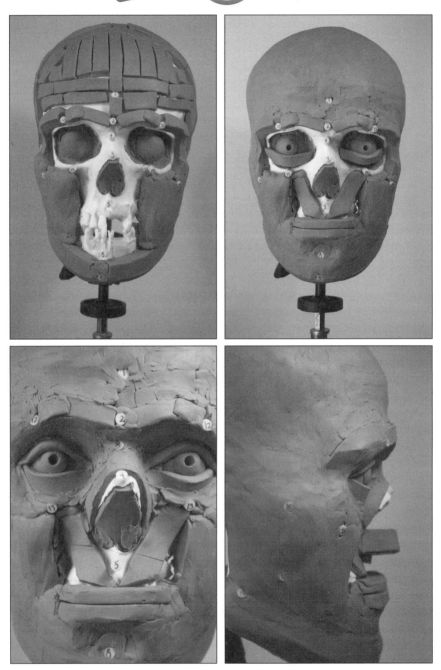

As the face slowly takes shape, Kristen relies on experience and intuition to help her create the three-dimensional portrait. Finishing off the sculpture, she adds the ears, nose, and lips, studying the underlying skull to make sure these features are as realistic as possible.

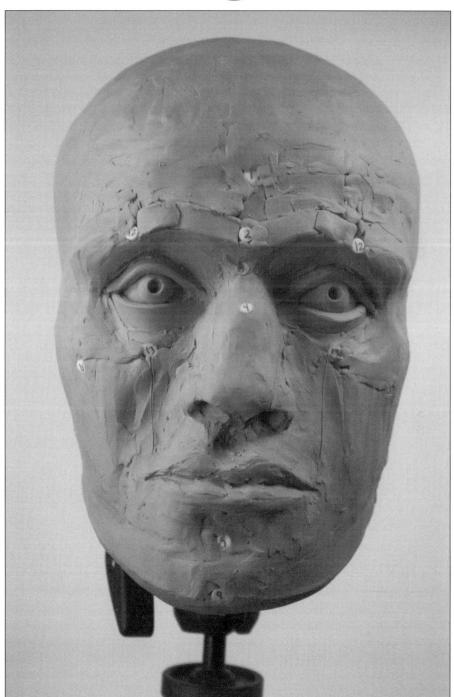

Skull with nose and eye detail.

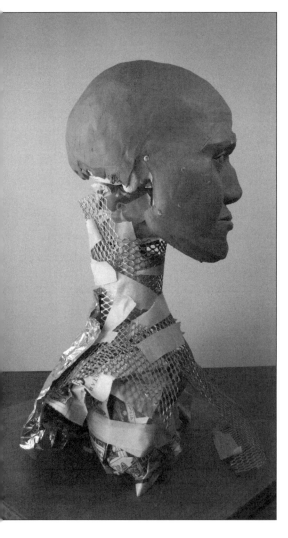

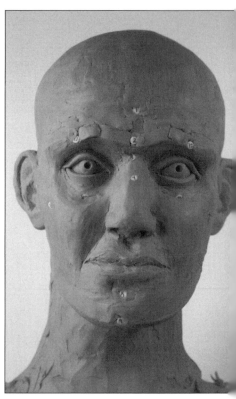

Kristen then creates a neck and upper chest for the structure, because she does not want it to look like a "floating head." She wants the sculpture to look as life-like as possible.

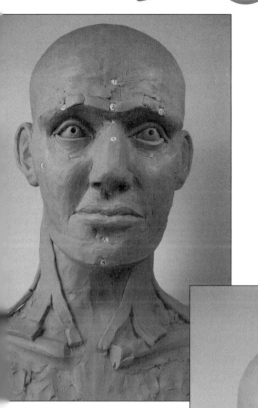

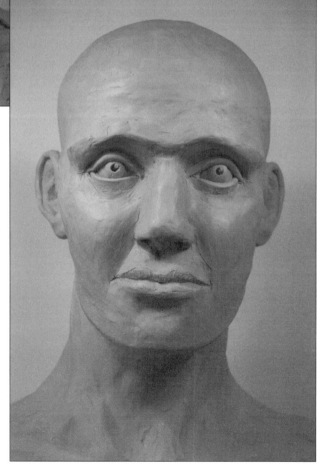

issing Persons Report

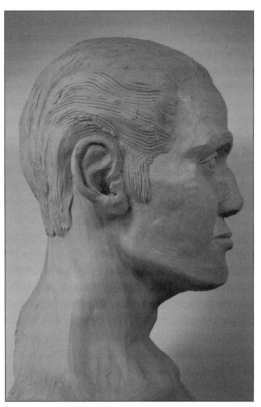

Lastly, she adds a simple hairstyle.
This sculpture is photographed at
many different angles.

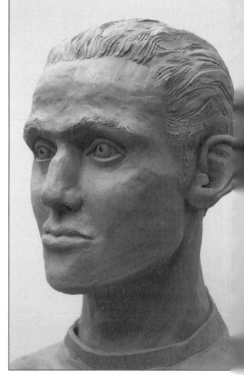

Finished
Reconstruction.

Kristen Freeborn with her finished reconstruction. Once, she and investigators are satisfied with the finished results, the sculpture is carefully taken apart and the skull returned to investigators. Kristen can create a 3-D sculpture even if the skull is not complete. By using her knowledge in anatomy and physiology she can create the "missing parts" of the skull.

Search Dogs

When Rita Argiros is not out with the dogs, she is running The Family School, a residential school for at-risk teens. It was her dedication to the school that got her interested in search dogs.

The Family School is located just outside of Hancock, New York, in the wilderness. Most of these youths do not choose to come to the school, they are placed there by families that are at their wit's end. As a result, many of these teens runaway; however, they are ill-equipped for the rugged and rural terrain surrounding the school. They often will runaway in some of the worst weather conditions. Rita would spend many nights worrying about these lost teens, sometimes fearing for their lives Then she read about dogs who could find lost people. After attending her first training, she was convinced this was something that not only would help her find these wayward children, but could be incorporated into the program at the school. When I visited, three of the students were actively involved in the day's training session.

Rita currently works with two dogs: Ripley and Raven, Ripley's daughter. They are friendly, playful animals that belie their heroic talents. On the day I visited Rita, Ripley, and the other Eagle Valley Search and Rescue members, it was an unseasonably warm January day, around 40 degrees, but the snow was still deep. The warm temperatures made the snow become heavy and slushy, not easy for walking. With Robin, a search and rescue volunteer, we drove about a quarter-mile on a dead-end road. Robin parked her truck on the side of the road, where we entered a seemingly endless tract of deep woods. We hiked up a steep incline, over a brook, and into the Catskill Mountains. The deep woods were shaded and it suddenly didn't feel as warm as it did in the sunshine. Though I was wearing layers and a down vest, I was not prepared to spend a long time out in the woods. When I expressed my concerns to Robin, she says, "Don't worry, Ripley will find us. We won't be out here more than twenty minutes."

Ripley is Rita Argiros' German Shepherd. He is not the handsome brown and black show dogs you see on television. He is a thin wiry, mostly black dog with huge ears. He prances around playfully, like a puppy, and would do anything for a ball. Even though I witnessed Ripley's skills earlier in the day, I am relying on this dog to find me in a heavily wooded area with night quickly approaching. Rita and Ripley do not know where we are. Just like in a real search, they have been given a general area that covers approximately one hundred acres. They did not watch me leave the area. They did not know if I left in a vehicle or on foot. They will not see where the truck is parked or have the advantage of following our footprints up the hill. Rita will rely solely on Ripley's leading to find us. It is three o'clock in the afternoon, the sun is beginning to set, and I am beginning to regret volunteering for this task. The search and rescue teams call these practice tasks "problems." Ripley is the only one that can solve this problem for me.

Rita Argiros and Ripley.

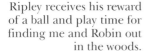issing Persons Report

I spread my vest on a frozen tree trunk and sat down with Robin to await Ripley. She radios to the base station that the targets (that's us) are in position. She is still smiling as she sits down next to me in the cold. I picture myself freezing to death.

Within minutes, I hear a clanging way off in the distance. It is the bell Ripley wears around his neck. I am amazed. It has been less than five minutes and Ripley's search started about a mile away over the top of a hill. In a real situation, I would have stood up and started calling to the dog, but not all victims are able to call out, so Robin and I hush, making it harder for Ripley to locate us. However, a few minutes later Ripley jumps over the log we are sitting on, gives us both a quick sniff, and run backs to Rita to signal he has found us. He stops, barks vigorously at Rita, and heads back to our location. He will do this as many times as necessary until she reaches our location. For practice, she pretends she doesn't see us and heads in another direction, but Ripley doesn't give up; he barks, redirecting her to our frozen log. So, what does Ripley get for this heroic effort? Rita pulls a ball from her pocket and Ripley begins to dance wildly around.

Ripley receives his reward of a ball and play time for finding me and Robin out in the woods.

Ripley is a non-discriminating scent dog. Sent out into the woods, Ripley will find any human being in the area, dead or alive. Some dogs are trained to discriminate and will look only for remains. These dogs are cadaver dogs. There are even dogs that are trained to search in and around water. These kinds of dogs are called air scent dogs. They do not follow any specific path or trail. Ripley can quickly "clear" hundreds of acres — that is, he can determine if any human is in the area. Air scent dogs are excellent workers when a person has gone missing in a wooded area. Rita tells me that, with experience, a good dog can even discriminate between the scents of the rescue workers and the lost subject.

Other dogs practicing that day with Ripley and the team are scent discriminating dogs or trailing dogs. These dogs are the one you see most often on television. They are given something to smell, such as an article of clothing, and then they will search only for that specific scent. A specific kind of trailing dog, called a tracking dog, will scent off a foot print and will only follow the track of that specific person. Tracking and trailing dogs will ignore all other scents and only look for the one they are given. Tracking and trailing dogs are best used when it is absolutely clear that the missing person has been in the area and is alone. Trailing and tracking dogs are often kept on leashes where as non-discriminating dogs run free with their handlers following. A tracking and trailing dog must be called in as soon as it is determined that a person is missing because the scent trail will quickly begin to deteriorate. Weather conditions can also cause the trail to deteriorate. Non-discriminating scent dogs can be called in any time to search (though the sooner the better).

A search dog can find a human being faster and more accurately than human searchers. Whereas a human searcher cannot always see under dense undergrowth or deep snow, the dog can scent exactly where a hidden human is. Rita tells me that Ripley can find human remains, the size of quarter, in a one hundred-acre area. No human searcher could do that. Even with flashlights, humans cannot search well at night. Specially trained search dogs can search day or night in any weather conditions. Rita and Ripley are trained to search at night. Ripley can search for six to seven hours before he needs a break for rest and food. With a well-planned, staggered search, a team of search dogs can search around the clock until the lost person is found or an area is clear and searchers are sure the lost person is not in the area.

Though search dogs can find human remains that have been in the area a long time, sometimes years' or decades' old, obviously, it is best to call in a search dog as soon it is determined a person is lost or missing. For a lost child, a person with dementia, a person who has indicated he/she may do harm to themselves, or extremely adverse weather conditions, a search team should be assembled immediately. Most police departments do not have search dogs and the few that do have only one or two. Volunteer search teams are always on alert and available any time, any day. They are free and do not cost the police or the family of the missing anything. While the desired result is that the search dog successfully locates a missing loved one, the search dog can also let the searchers know that an area is "clear" — that is, the missing person is not in the area. In that way, searchers can concentrate their efforts in more likely places. While most search teams will only work on police request, the family of the missing can discuss the possibility with the police or directly with the search teams to figure out the best way to conduct missing person searches.

Part Five

An Ounce of Prevention is Worth a Pound of Cure

In the summer of 2005, my fiancé decided he could no longer face life, left a suicide note, and disappeared. He walked out the door, not telling me or anyone else his destination. It was terrifying. That is how quickly someone can become an endangered missing person. Gripped by a deep fear, I did not know what to do. I called his best friend who advised me to call the police. It was the right advice. I called the police and they arrived at my home within minutes. Since he had threatened to kill himself, he was immediately considered endangered missing — a missing person whose life is in imminent danger — and a search began immediately. This is not always the way a search for a missing person begins. I was lucky in an odd sort of way, because of my fiancé's threat to kill himself, police were able to take immediate action and, because of this, he was located before he did any harm to himself and was able to get the treatment he needed. However, while I sat in my living room with investigators, I realized how little we really know about our loved ones and how precious minutes, if not hours or days, could be lost by our lack of preparedness for just such an emergency.

Missing Persons Report

No one believes that his or her loved one can become missing, but they do and it happens quickly. We get ready for other possible emergencies in our lives; many of us have candles on hand in case the electricity fails, we teach children how to dial 9-1-1, we install smoke detectors and practice safe routes to get out of our home in case of fire, but very few people are prepared for a loved one who goes missing. My fiancé was found quickly, within hours, but the sad truth was that I was little help in finding him. As the police asked me simple questions, such as his license plate number, his social security number, or even for a recent picture, I was unable to provide any of this. I didn't have the home number of any of his close friends or family because he kept this information in his cell phone, which he had with him. I felt lost and helpless. However, we can all be prepared for this kind of emergency. Everyone can create a "safe box" for each family member. It takes a little effort to complete the safe box, but once you have done so, you can simply update it yearly. Creating a safe box — gathering and keeping information about family members — can be useful, if not pivotal, in emergency situations. Hopefully, you will never use a safe box, but in the extreme case you have to, it can save precious time.

Putting Together
a Safe Box

Every family member should have a "safe box." A safe box is a small, secure, storage space where important information about each family member is kept. You can buy a lockbox if you want to keep the information secure, but even a shoebox or those plastic "drawers" could be labeled and used for each family member. If you choose a box that locks, make sure the key is available to several family members. It is no good to have a safe box if the information cannot be accessed quickly. Make sure your safe box is kept in your home. It should not be kept elsewhere, such as a bank safe deposit box. Your safe box must be immediately and easily accessible in case of an emergency. Other family members should know where the safe box is kept and be able to access it in case of an emergency. If I had a safe box when my fiancé disappeared, it would have been as simple as handing the box over to the police investigators and they would have had enough information to begin their initial search.

Elements of the Safe Box

Recent Photos

You should always have a recent photo of every family member. You should have a close-up and a full-body shot. It's easy to do for children, as they get a school picture each year, but don't forget about adults. This could be a ritual you set up on a birthday. On the back of the picture you should write the date the picture was taken, nicknames, eye and hair color, birth date, and any other identifying marks such as tattoos or piercings. If your family member has a tattoo, you will want a close-up picture of the tattoo.

Full names and phone numbers of friends

While this is important for all family members, it is especially important for teenagers. It is surprising the number of parents who do not know the last names of their children's school friends, where they live, or their phone numbers. Get this information at the beginning of each school year or when your child makes a new friend. However, don't forget about all the adults. This is also particularly important for adults who live alone. You should list all your regular contacts with their phone numbers and addresses. An address book or a journal is a good place to do this.

Screen Names and Passwords for All Computer Programs

You may need to access e-mail or a person's computer files quickly. You absolutely need passwords for e-mail and social networks. Teens may be hesitant to give you this information. It is up to you how to handle your own teenager, but in general, if you trust your teens you can ask them to keep this information on a 3x5 card and put it somewhere you can have immediate access to. You can agree to only access this information in an emergency. However, don't forget to get this information from adults, too.

Fingerprint cards

You can get fingerprint cards from at your local police department. The police often run programs for children where you can get a card you keep of your children's fingerprints. When you get your children's fingerprints, ask for extra cards for the adults in your family. Fingerprints *do not change* so they are good forever. You can also take fingerprints on a piece of white cardboard. Get the cardboard used for making ink stamp cards. Have a separate card for each family member. Write the person's name, birth date, and social security number on the back of the card.

Social Security Number

Photocopy the card of each family member and keep the copy in the safebox.

Copies of Driver License and Vehicle Registrations

This may sound silly, but many people don't remember their license plate number. I certainly didn't when my fiancé went missing. Yes, the police can "look it up," but it is good to have it handy.

Contact Name and Numbers of Employers

You should also get a home phone number for each family member's immediate supervisor. If a person doesn't arrive home from work, and the business is closed, you will want to be able to contact someone other than at the place of employment.

Missing Persons Report

Contact Number of Other Family Members

This is important if a child does not live with both parents. The police will need the name, address, and phone number of the other parent immediately. You will also want to have contact numbers of grandparents and any other family members who have regular contact with your child.

Emergency Contact for School Personnel

I came home late one day from work to find a phone call on my answering machine. It indicated that my fifteen-year-old daughter had not shown up for school that day. It was almost five o'clock, school was closed, and no one answered any of the many numbers I dialed. I was panicked. Luckily, it was just a mix up and my daughter arrived home on the late bus, but today with parents working it is good to know emergency numbers to reach school personnel if the school is closed. Ask for these numbers. The school should be willing to provide you with one administrator's number that you can use in case of an emergency.

A List of All Medical Conditions and Medications Family Members Have/Take

Doctor's Contact Information

This is particularly important if a family member has a medical condition (see above).

Every Family Member's Cell Phone Number

You should also have directions on how to access voice-mail from another phone. Don't forget to write down the password for the voice-mail. You may need to access the voice-mail and you should be able to do that from any phone.

Bank Account and Credit Card Information

Be sure to notify the bank if a loved one goes missing. The bank can contact you immediately if any of the accounts are accessed. If the person has online bank accounts and/or can access credit card accounts from online, have the password for each account.

Get a Copy of Each Family Member's DNA

This is easy and quick. Start by using a cotton swab in the inside of the mouth of every family member. Run the swab around inside the mouth for two minutes. Place this swab in a freezer-safe baggie, put the person's name and social security number on the outside of this bag, and place the bag in the freezer. Use a separate bag for each family member. It will keep as long as it is kept frozen. However, I refresh this bag at least once a year.

Keep Your Safe Box Secure But Accessible

Obviously, the information in the safe box is sensitive and private. Find a secure place to store it. However, close family members need to know where the box is and how to access it in case of an emergency.

Remember to update your safe box at least once a year. Set a specific date for this so you will remember: a birthday or a holiday. Some people think a "safe box" is being paranoid, but it's not. Once you have a safe box in place, you don't have to think about it or worry. It is no different than any other emergency planning, such as smoke detectors or making sure your family understands how to get out of the house in case of a fire.

~~~~~

Hopefully, you will never have to use the safebox information, but if you do, it could save precious time. The sooner after a disappearance the police can begin an effective search, the more likely the person will be recovered safely.

Other Things You Can Do To Stay Safe

Always Let Someone Know Where You Are

We often remember to do this for the most vulnerable people, such as the elderly and children, but everyone should have a person that he or she contacts on a regular basis. Have a family member or a friend that you call or send an e-mail to at least once a week. If you are going away, tell someone where you are going. Agree to contact them when you get there and when you leave. When I travel, I leave behind a "safe card." My safe card is a large file card that says where I am going, complete with anticipated travel routes, and the names, phone numbers, and addresses of people I plan to meet. It does not mean you can't be flexible. A simple phone call or e-mail can tell family and friends you have changed your plans. If you are a hiker, it is very important to leave behind your plans. Always sign-in to trail books when you hike.

Don't Leave Home Without ID

Even if you are just going for a walk around the block, you should always have some form of ID on you. If you should get injured, it is imperative that rescue personnel be able to identify you and notify your loved ones.

Get in the Habit of Locking Doors in Your Home and Car

We all just "run into the store" for a minute and think we will be safe. This is the opportunity criminals look for. Locking your doors is a habit. Get used to doing it. Make sure all family members have a key to the doors and leave a key with a trusted friend or neighbor. Also, if it appears someone has broken into your car or house, do not enter. Leave the area, go to a safe place, and call the police.

Protect Your Personal Information

This is true in person or online. Never give out personal information to someone you do not know. In a business situation, do not give out information until you understand why it is needed, how it will be used, and how it will be protected.

Until You Know Someone Well, Agree Only to Meet in Public Places

Never get into a car with someone you do not know well. Make agreements to go to parties with friends and leave with the same friends. You can't stress this enough with teens.

Carry a cell phone.

If You Feel Uncomfortable in a Situation, Leave Immediately and Call for Help

We often feel we have to be nice to people. However, you do not have to help people or give directions to people if you feel uncomfortable. Use your cell phone if you see a disabled car. Trust your gut. If you are in an area or a situation and you feel unsafe, leave the area and go to a safe place. If this is not possible, use your cell phone and call for help.

Educate All Members of Your Family

Everyone in the family should know what to do if they are in danger of being abducted. Oftentimes schools have these programs for children. Talk to children about what they learn and most importantly *practice* what to do. However, adults need to learn what to do in case of their own abduction. Everyone, children and adults alike, should know what to do if they become lost. Use the sources listed here and take some awareness courses.

Part Six

When a Loved One
Goes Missing...

When a person goes missing, those left behind can experience a wide range of emotions: anger, shock, denial, shame, and fear. In the beginning, when a person first goes missing, there is a lot of chaos and commotion; phone calls, police visits, searching, questions, family and friends stopping by for support, etc. However, the longer a person is missing, the quieter things seem to become. As the police move on to solve other crimes and life moves on, the loved ones feel a deep sense of frustration. They are left with a giant hole in their lives and the world just doesn't seem to care. They don't know where to turn. This section of the book is to help family members and loved ones to continue the search.

No one is alone. When a loved one goes missing, those left behind can learn from those who have walked that path before them. Kalli J. Lee, a woman involved in coordinating the search for Kellisue Ackernecht, has decided that she will do one thing a day, no matter how small, to bring Kellisue home. This section can help you with the initial search, and if necessary, a longer search. Here are a list of suggestions and sources that you can use to do one thing a day.

What To Do Right Away

As difficult as it will be, when investigators arrive, the person who discovered the disappearance or who knows the most should sit and work with investigators. This would be the time to have the safe box handy to give to investigators.

When my fiancé went missing, the police asked me to stay with them, answer questions, provide information, and continue to try to phone him every fifteen minutes. They were hoping that when he heard my voice he would give some hints to his location. They also hoped that if he turned his phone on (it was turned off), they could trace it and locate him. It was very hard to stay home while other people looked for him, but I knew what I was doing was very important.

The police may ask very intrusive and/or embarrassing questions. Do not take offense to this. They do not know you or the missing person and are simply trying to build a profile and get clues to the causes of the disappearance. Answer honestly. Your house may also suddenly seem to be overrun by people in uniform. When my fiancé disappeared, police from three agencies arrived. You may ask them what they are doing, but they are there to look for clues and get information. People disappear under all sorts of circumstances and the police must figure out what happened.

When You Realize A Loved One Is Missing...

Call the Police

The first thing you should do, if you think a loved one has gone missing, is call the police. Sometimes people hesitate to do this. What if he is at a friend's house? What if she simply forgot to call? What if he told me where he'd be and I forgot? These are all doubts that pop into a person's head. We want to stay in denial because the alternative is terrifying. However, keep in mind the sooner you call the police, the sooner a search can commence and the chances that the missing person will be found quickly increases dramatically. If a person who has always been reliable suddenly misses something important, such as work, a family gathering, or an appointment, you should check immediately for him or her. Go to his house. Call his employer. Call her friends. However, don't let too much time elapse. Once you think you have checked thoroughly, do not hesitate to call the police. If the person has threatened to kill him/herself, don't wait to call the police. Don't even "check around." If a person is contemplating suicide, a search must begin immediately.

Check Where You Think the Person Might Be

While you are waiting for investigators to arrive, you should look everywhere you believe the person could possibly be, particularly if you are looking for a child. Look in closets, basements, attics, crawl spaces, appliances, and any place that the person might fit. Outside make sure you check cars, particularly the trunk, under porches, in storage sheds, in the shrubbery, and in any abandoned appliances. Inform neighbors immediately of the situation and ask them to help.

Get on the Phone

While other people are physically searching for the missing person, call everyone who may have had contact with the missing person that day. Check his or her home, call the employer and ask when he or she was last there. Contact all of their friends and family. It's okay if it is late at night or early in the morning; this is an emergency. Don't wait. Call the bank and credit card companies to alert them. They can watch the missing person's account for any activity. Do the same for the person's cell phone.

Get on the Computer

Sign on to the missing person's computer and read e-mails and check social networking sites. Go to all the sites the missing person has under the "favorite" heading on the home page. In the search engine, use the drop down tab to see all the sites the person visits frequently.

File a Missing Person Report

If the police are hesitant to take one, be insistent. Provide the police with as much information as you can. Explain clearly why you believe your loved one is missing and simply isn't off somewhere and has lost track of time. My fiancé told me he was planning to kill himself and what to tell his sons after his death. I gave this information to the police immediately so they knew that my fiancé was not just somewhere "blowing off steam," but he had made a direct threat to his own life. If you think your loved one is in danger, let the police know. Don't worry if you feel you are relaying rumors, suspicion, or hearsay. It is the police's job to investigate.

Answer the Police's Questions As Fully As You Can

The police will begin by asking questions and lots of them. It will be difficult to answer them for two reasons. One reason, is that you will be so worried you may have difficulty focusing. It is okay to ask another family member or friend to help you out. The second reason is that you will want to be out looking for your missing loved one. Remember, answer police questions may be key in finding your loved one. Leave the search to others in the beginning. It is also okay to ask family and friends to make phone calls and start searching. I had called all of my fiancé's family and friends and they were out looking in all the places they could think of.

Keep Track of the Investigation

Your house may quickly become a center for the search. Police from several agencies may arrive at your house. This happened in my case. The local police from several agencies, The New York State Police, and even police from the Department of Environmental Conservation arrived at my home. One office was assigned to stay with me at all times. I don't know if this was because I was a suspect, to get as much information as he could from me, or just to comfort me, but I liked having someone there, knowing he was there to help. I knew instinctively to write down everyone's name who was involved in the search. Police carry business cards now. Ask for them. If you forget, you can ask for them later. You never know when you may have a question for someone who was involved with the search. Keep a diary, this can just be a notebook, and write in it often, at least once a day if the investigation lasts longer than a few days. You may not think to do all this right away. Don't worry. It is better to start a little late than not at all.

Allow the Police to Search

The police asked if they could search my home. Of course, this feels uncomfortable, but I knew the police might find something I overlooked because they are trained to do so. Let the police do their job. Of course, you do not have to allow any police agency to search your home without a warrant. I had nothing to hide and knew that the police were only doing their job to help find my fiancé.

issing Persons Repo

Tell the Truth

It is important to tell the truth. It was extremely difficult to tell the police that my fiancé and I had a fight just before he left. I felt like I was sharing deeply personal and intimate parts of my life. However, when creating a profile of the missing person and the circumstances of his/her disappearance, it is important to give the police the complete picture. You may even feel the police are accusing you of something, I certainly did. However, I knew it was important to rule out other scenarios so they could focus on finding my fiancé.

Ask questions

If you are not sure what to do, ask. "What would you like me to do?" I asked. The police told me that they wanted me to stay by the phone in case my fiancé called. They also wanted me to continue to try to reach his cell phone once every fifteen minutes with the hopes that he would answer. Do what the police ask you to do. It may be difficult. I certainly did not want to stay put, but I knew I was doing what needed to be done.

If Your Loved One
is Not Recovered
Right Away...

Make a Decision About the Media

Eventually, the decision has to be made about the media. It is best to try to do this in conjunction with the police. In the case of abductions the police will want to get the information out to the media as quickly as possible. Some reporters are wonderfully open, generous people who truly want to help. I find this to be the case more often than not, but reporters are not the police. Ask the police prior to talking to the media what it is okay to tell the media and what isn't. You do not want to jeopardize the search.

Create A Missing Person's Flyer to Post

There are organizations that can also help you do this (see the "Source Book" section). Fax the missing person flyers to all media outlets and police agencies in your area. Ask businesses to hang up the flyer. Hanging flyers is something friends can do when they want to help.

Assign One Person to be Primary Contact for the Family in the Investigation

Usually this is the missing person's parent, spouse, or other close family member. You will want to make sure all information is going through one person. You do not want to have bits and pieces collected by different people. Sometimes, the family may also want to assign someone to act as the media liaison. Speaking to the media can be difficult and emotional, particularly for a family that isn't used to being in the limelight. Choosing one person who feels comfortable with speaking to the public can take pressure off everyone else.

Continue to Work Closely With the Police

It's easy to become frustrated and feel the police aren't doing enough to get your loved one home. While the police will keep you updated, sometimes they cannot share all the information they have or it will jeopardize the investigation. However, at any time if you feel the police are not taking your case seriously, you can ask to speak to a supervisor or even your local district attorney.

Contact NamUS, Open a Case File, and Give a DNA Sample

NamUS is a data based created by the U.S. Department of Justice to match unidentified remains with those of missing persons (see listing in this book). However, it does more than just match. Many people use NamUS and may see your missing person listing and contact authorities.

Get Help

You are not alone. Listed in the "Sources Book" section are organizations that can help you get through this difficult time. These organizations can help you with every part of the search. You are not the first person to go through this. Other people, who have lived through similar experiences can help you, guide you and give you advice.

Part Seven

Doing the
Right Thing

"The world is a dangerous place, not because of those who do evil, but because of those who look on and do nothing." ~ Albert Einstein

When a person goes missing, the people left behind suffer. The suffering I have witnessed is indescribable. It destroys people from the inside out. It breaks up families, causes depression, anger, and loneliness. It destroys lives and robs people of their own lives. Even people who successfully manage the loss of a loved one still suffer. The most inhumane thing a person can do is to witness human suffering, have the means to relieve it, and do nothing.

In general, it is believed that in the cases for most missing people, someone knows something. Maybe someone noticed that a neighbor hasn't been around in a very long while or a family that used to have a child no longer has that child. After thinking about it, something that seemed small or insignificant may actually be the clue investigators are looking for. Or a person may have witnessed something more substantial, saw or heard something out of the ordinary, or they may have actually witnessed part of or all of a crime, not realizing at the time it was a crime. He may have overheard a conversation or heard someone bragging, even though it may have sounded unbelievable at the time. At the very worse, a person may actually have been involved in an incident where a person was harmed or abducted. He or she may not have intended to harm the person — maybe it was a fight gone wrong. If this is the case, then it's time to do the right thing.

If you think you know something about a missing person, it is your obligation to give that information to authorities so they can follow up on it. You may think what you know is too small or insignificant. You may not even be sure it pertains to the missing person. You may think you are just being a busybody. However small the information or evidence is, just give it to the police. It is their job to follow-up on it and decide whether it is relevant or not. Once you have given your information to the police, then you can rest easier knowing you have done the right thing. Cases are frequently solved when a person comes forward with information he or she thought was insignificant.

If you think you have important information, all you have to do is simply call the police. They will send someone to meet you and discuss what you know. If you do not want the police to come to your home, you can always go to the police department or arrange to meet them at another location. Many people are afraid of law enforcement officers. They believe they will become a suspect. That is not the case. Most law enforcement officials who work on cases involving the missing are very professional, hard-working, and kind individuals.

If you think you have found evidence, such as a piece of clothing or identification, it is important that you do not touch it or move it. You should leave it at the location where you found it and call the police immediately. However, if you did touch it or move it — for example, you were cleaning up the side of the road and found something and only after you picked it up did you realized it might be important — simply put it back and explain to the police exactly where you found it. It is human nature to bend down to pick something up to see what it is. The police realize that.

If You Are A Witness

Being a witness is a scary thing. You may think that no one will believe you if you come forward. Worse yet, you may fear that your life will be in danger if you come forward. Maybe you have been raised with the philosophy "snitched get stitches." The good news is that in many cases you can give information to law enforcement agencies anonymously. Although bringing an abductor to justice is important, it is more important to locate the missing person.

Many people don't realize that communication between a lawyer and a client is confidential. Only the client has the power to waive confidentiality. If you have some important information, you can hire an attorney and give the attorney permission to release that information to the proper authorities, without using your identity. In this manner, if the authorities have questions or need clarification, they can work through your attorney. Even if you don't want to remain anonymous, I strongly suggest you consult an attorney before you contact authorities with information. An attorney knows the legal system and can give you advice. If you don't have the money to hire an attorney, you can contact your county's Legal Aid office. Legal Aid provides free or reduced legal advice to people who cannot afford it.

Consulting with a therapist or a minister can be another option to help you come forward. Just remember, these avenues may not always protect your identity. Check with the minister or therapist before revealing any sensitive or confidential information. Tell the therapist or minister that you are a witness or were involved in a crime without giving the specifics. The minister or therapist will tell you their legal obligations before you continue. If you decide to work with a minister or therapist, the good thing about pursuing this avenue is the minister or therapist can give you the emotional support you need while making your decision to do the right thing. They can refer you to the proper professionals who can advise you on how to proceed with the information you have.

Often times, there are hotline numbers or "tip lines" for people to call. You can always call these numbers from a payphone or a pre-paid cell phone if you want to remain anonymous. If you are going to do this, I recommend that you sit down and write down everything you want to say before you call so you won't forget anything. Please be as specific and detailed as you can when you call in. Don't be afraid. These really are anonymous tip-lines. Yes, the dispatcher may ask you for your name, but simply tell the dispatcher that you are giving this information anonymously. The police are really just trying to get all the information they can to help them find the missing person.

If You Were Involved

If you are involved in a crime, see a lawyer immediately. Don't wait for the police to "come to you." Remember, recovering the missing person is the most important factor in these cases. You can end a lot of suffering by helping to locate a missing person. Your lawyer can give you all the advice you need. You may pass along information through a lawyer without turning yourself in. However, if you decide to turn yourself in, your lawyer can advise you the best way to go about it. If you cannot afford a lawyer, contact your county's legal aid office. Just remember, you are doing the right thing.

issing Persons Repo

If You Are the Missing Person

... And Do NOT Want to be Found

If you are the "missing person," and have left on your own accord, please contact the police immediately. If you do NOT want to be found, tell this to the police. The police may not release any information about your whereabouts if you are a legal adult and have left on your own. If you are a runaway and under eighteen years old, call the National Runaway Hotline (1-800-runaway). This is a confidential hotline. By letting people know you are alive and well — and not wanting to be found — the police can stop looking for you and not waste precious time and resources on someone who is not in danger. However, I strongly recommend you contact whoever is looking for you. You can do this through an anonymous letter or phone call; just tell them you are fine and simply do not want to be found. The police will pass on information for you if you ask them to. You can tell the police to tell your family that you are fine and do not want to be found. Though they may still be upset that you don't want to come home, at least it will give your family some comfort to know you are alive and well.

... And Want to go Home or Reconnect With Your Loved Ones

If you believe you are considered a "missing person," you should contact the police. Perhaps you just went off on your own and now want to reconnect with your family. Maybe you were sick and now remember things you didn't before. Or perhaps you were abducted as a child by a non-custodial parent. Even if you are not sure, the police can work with you to confirm or deny your suspicions. If you have been missing, countless hours, manpower, time, and materials have been invested in your disappearance...not to mention the huge emotional impact. If you *aren't* a missing person, it is usually very quick and easy to confirm that your suspicions aren't true. Don't be embarrassed. It is the job of the police to investigate. Proving things aren't true is a very important part of law enforcement, too.

issing Persons Report

If you believe you may have been abducted as a child and are now grown, you have several avenues to pursue. The most important thing to remember is if you were abducted, people have been looking for you for a very long time. This will be a difficult time for you, particularly if you were abducted by a parent, family member, or someone who has cared for you. You may not want a loved one to go to jail, but know that any consequences resulting from your abduction are not your fault. A person chose to abduct you, and whatever the consequences of that abduction, they have nothing to do with you reconnecting with the people who love you and have been searching for you for a very long time. The situation cannot be resolved if you do not come forward. Someone has been suffering for years and just knowing you are alive and well will end that suffering. I can assure you, someone *is* looking for you and his or her life has been torn to shreds because of your absence. Only you can start the healing process.

For all missing people who want to reconnect, the best place to start is by contacting a lawyer, minister, or therapist. They can steer you to the right organizations, authorities, and people to help while offering you support. If you are sure you were abducted, you can check with the National Center for Missing and Exploited Children. They can give you advice and help you to reunite with your family.

Source Book

T his section is a Source Book, a type of resource guide, for people who either have a missing loved one or would like to become part of the effort to help locate the missing.

The Center for Hope

20 Prospect Street, Suite 103, Chocolate Factory
Ballston Spa, NY 12020

WEBSITE: www.hope4themissing.org
E-MAIL: jdlmary@hope4themissing.org
PHONE: 518-884-8761

The Center for Hope was created by Joe and Mary Lyall after the disappearance of their daughter, Suzanne. The Lyalls knew that keeping hope alive is the most important part of the search for their daughter. Without hope, people become paralyzed by anger and frustration. The Center for Hope is a nonprofit organization that can assist and support family and friends through the entire search process. The Center for Hope hosts a New York State Missing Person's Conference each year in April for family, friends and supporters of missing persons. I would strongly recommend you attend the yearly conference if you have a missing loved one. It will help you network with people you might not otherwise have met. The website lists many sources for the family and friends of the missing. It also has a flyer creation program so you can create a missing person's flyer to distribute.

issing Persons Report

New York State Missing and Exploited Clearing House

New York State Division of Criminal Justice Services, 4 Tower Place, Albany, NY 12203-3764

WEBSITE: www.criminaljustice.state.ny.us/missing
E-MAIL: missingchildren@dcjs.state.ny.us
PHONE: 1-800-FIND-KID

If your child or some child you know is missing in New York State, this website has a wide range of helpful information. It is part of the New York State Department of Criminal Justice Services. You can find information on missing children, runaways, New York State Laws regarding missing persons and educational resources. Along with support for families, it also sponsors community education programs. If you are interested in starting programs in your community this is a good place to start. Most importantly, the site provides a link where anyone who has information on a missing child can submit a lead.

National Center for Missing Adults

LBTH/NCMA, PO BOX 19,
Bentonville, AR, 72712

HOTLINE: 1-800-690-FIND
E-MAIL: info@missingadults.org

The National Center for Missing Adults offers resources to the families of endangered missing adults. This site also acts as a clearinghouse for information about missing adults. If you are interested in bringing safety education programs for children and adults into your community NCMA can assist you in this. As well as families, this site can also provide information to law enforcement agencies. The Center is in the process of creating support groups to help the families of the missing. The best part of the NCMA is the resources listed.

National Runaway Switchboard

3080 N. Lincoln Avenue, Chicago, IL 60657

WEBSITE: www.1800RUNAWAY.org
CRISIS HOTLINE: 1-800-RUNAWAY

The National Runaway Switchboard was established in 1971, as a response to runaway children in Chicago. It is now a federally funded, national communication system for our nation's homeless and runaway children. Along with helping bring children home, the hotline offers help to families with crisis intervention referrals to local organizations to help the family reunite and stay together. It also can help families with education and runaway prevention. If you believe your missing child may be a runaway, you should contact this hotline right away. They can refer you to resources in your local area to help in the search, recovery, and homecoming of your child. All calls are free, anonymous, and confidential.

The Charley Project

WEBSITE: www.charleyproject.org
CONTACT: Meaghan Good
EMAIL: administrator@charleyproject.com

The Charley Project began as website and source for the missing. It is an attempt to compile all the people missing in the United States into one central database. Amazingly, the site is run entirely by one person, Meaghan Good. As such, it is a database only. The site was originally founded by Jennifer Marra, who also founded The Doe Network. In 2003, Jennifer handed control of the website to Meaghan, who renamed the site. The site was named after Charley Brewster, who was abducted when he was four years old from Germantown, Pennsylvania, in 1874. Charley was never recovered even though his family spent the rest of their lives searching for him. Meaghan has dedicated her site not only to Charlie, but to all the missing, so they will never be forgotten. Since the Charley Project is a database only, it offers few resources. However, it is the most comprehensive list of missing Americans, therefore everyone should make sure their missing loved one is listed on this site. Please check the site for the criteria for listing a missing person.

The Doe Network

121 Short Street, Livingston, TN 38570

WEBSITE: www.doenetwork.org
CONTACT: Todd Matthews
PHONE: 931-397-3893
FAX: 931-823-9821

The Doe Network is a volunteer organization. The volunteers spend countless hours scouring the news and internet looking for tips and leads help law enforcement solve cold cases. They deal only with cold cases in which the individual disappeared prior to 1999 and unidentified decedents whose death is believed to have occurred prior to 2006. The site lists the cases of hundreds of missing people on their website in hopes that this information may prompt someone to come forward with tips or clues. Their volunteers also spend countless hours looking for connections between unidentified remains and missing people in the hopes of making a match. The Network also works closely with the media to share information on the missing and unidentified. If you are interested in helping finding missing persons, contact this site. If you missing loved one fits the sites criteria, please contact them to have your missing loved one listed.

NamUS

National and Unidentified Missing Persons System

WEBSITE: www.namus.gov
E-MAIL: questions@findthemissing.org
*If you have questions about a specific case, use the website and click on the contact information for the Case Manager or Regional Systems Administrator for the case in question.

The United States Department of Justice has created a data-base called National Missing and Unidentified Missing Persons System (NamUS). The goal of NamUs is to compare unidentified remains with those of missing persons with the hopes of finding matches and returning the missing to their loved ones. According to the NamUs website it is estimated that there are currently 40,000 unidentified remains around

the United States. Every single one of those unidentified remains is a missing person and someone is looking for him/her.

NamUs has two searchable databases. The first is the Unidentified Person's Database and the other is the Missing Person's Database. The Unidentified Person's Database lists information that is entered by medical examiners, coroners and other agencies. The listings are for people who have died under any circumstance and could not be identified by traditional means. Anyone can search this database for his/her missing loved one. If you find a potential match, you can request information regarding your missing loved one be sent to the agencies that holds the remains.

The Missing Person's Database contains missing person information. This information can be entered by anyone, however, NamUs will verify all the information before creating a listing. This database can also help provide missing person's posters, maps of possible travel routes to help searchers and provides links to other valuable organizations. NamUs can provide families with free DNA testing and forensic services. If you are a family member of a missing person contact NamUs. Someone will help you gather and record all the information you need to create a case file on the system. You may also request the agency coordinating the search effort of your missing loved one to become actively involved in registering on the NamUs website

While NamUs is potentially a powerful tool to match the missing with the unidentified it is currently a voluntary system. There are no laws that require law enforcement agencies to report the missing to NamUs. As of July 2010, NamUs only lists 4668 open missing persons cases and 6767 unidentified persons. Though woefully inadequate is a start. I urge you to contact your state and federal representative to make registration in NamUs a requirement for all people missing under mysterious or endangered circumstances and all unidentified remains.

National Crime Information Center (NCIC)

**Criminal Justice Information Services (CJIS) Division,
1000 Custer Hollow Road,
Clarksburg, WV 26306**

PHONE: (304) 625-2000

The NCIC is a database of criminal justice information administered by the FBI. As such, it keeps records of missing persons and unidentified remains. It also keeps a list of unidentified persons who are still alive. This is one of the only databases where unidentified alive persons are recorded. This database is accessible to law enforcement and other governmental agencies. The FBI will list all persons who are missing under mysterious or dangerous circumstances. Registration into the NCIC database is voluntary and must be done by a police or governmental agency. If you are the family of a missing person, request that your local agency list your missing person with NCIC. You will receive a case number after registration.

Mission Possible Investigations

P.O. Box 5564, Albany, NY 12205

WEBSITE: www.mpinvestigations.net
E-MAIL: jrichardson@mpinvestigations.com
PHONE: 518-702-1219
FAX: 509-753-1219

Deciding to hire a private investigator can be a very difficult decision. However, Jamie Richardson, founder of Mission Possible Investigations and Stacey Jones, investigator, can be a great service to the families of the missing. Jamie is a former Marine with a background in missing persons, elder abuse, and civil and criminal investigations. Stacy has a background in missing persons, child abuse, sexual assault and domestic violence. They can give you a free consultation and tell you what they, or any other private investigator, can or cannot, do for you. They will give you a fee schedule upfront and provide for you an accounting of all the time they spend on searching for your missing loved one. They are fully licensed, evidence they recover is admissible in a court of law and they work closely with police investigators.

Eagle Valley Search and Rescue

CONTACT: Rita Argiros
PHONE: 845-887-4679
E-MAIL: info@evdogs.org

Eagle Valley Search and Rescue team is a Catskill and Upper Delaware River Valley dog search team that searches for lost and missing persons. The highly trained team of searchers and dogs are available free of charge. In general, the team does not take requests from individuals and work only with investigating agencies. The dogs can assist in trailing, area searches, human remains detection and water recovery. You may contact Rita Argiros directly for assistance in planning a search

Kristen Freeborn,
Forensic Artist

60 East Street, Fort Edward, NY 12828

WEBSITE: www.forensicskullreconstruction.com
E-MAIL: Kristen_Freeborn@yahoo.com
PHONE: 518-796-5759

Kristen Freeborn is a gifted freelance forensic artist who can create composite drawings, 2-D and 3-D forensic facial reconstruction and age progressions. She will work for investigating agencies or directly for families of the missing. If you have a loved one who has been missing for a long time, contact Kristen with creating an updated image.

Hiring
a Private Investigator

S ome families become frustrated during the investigation by police into the disappearance of their loved one. This is quite common. For one thing, the missing person case will not be the only case the detective is working on and, as time goes by, the detective will have less and less time to dedicate to the search. Keep in mind, this does not mean that detectives are not doing their jobs. By and large, detectives are dedicated professionals who give many hours to solving their cases. Most detectives take missing person cases personally and dedicate many off-hours to the search. However, sometimes the family believes hiring someone to dedicate serious time and effort to the search is the best course of action. Like other decisions in the search for a missing loved one, the decision to hire a private investigator should be made carefully. Please use these guidelines for selecting a private investigator.

1. You should never make this decision out of frustration or anger. Unfortunately, I have far too many stories from families of unscrupulous investigators who took their money, but never offered any clues into the location of their missing loved one. Think and plan carefully. Interview more than one private investigator.

2. Start your search with the detectives who are working on your missing loved one's case. Most detectives understand the family's desire to bring in outside help and are cooperative. They can give you a suggested list of names of investigators.

3. Check with organizations that assist families of the missing. They can give you a list of investigators who have helped other families.

4. Ask your lawyer for a referral. Lawyers use investigators routinely and can usually give you names of investigators they have used.

Missing Persons Report

5. Interview several investigators before choosing one. A good investigator will not charge for an initial consultation. Do not rush the process.

6. Check with the state to make sure the investigator you have chosen is licensed. Never hire an investigator who does not have a current license.

7. Visit the investigator in his or her office the first time. If the investigator does not have an office, that is a sure sign he may not be legitimate.

8. Ask for references and then *check* them. The investigator you choose should have a good, solid background in law enforcement.

9. If the investigator contacts you out of the blue or is pressuring you to hire him or her, walk away. A good investigator does not need to contact clients out of the blue or push people into hiring him or her. No investigator should be offering you a guarantee that they will find your loved one. There is no guarantee. If the offer sounds too good, it is too good. However, sometimes an investigator may say you can get some of your money back if he or she is unable to find any new evidence. That is an acceptable agreement. Remember, that a private investigator is not a miracle worker. The investigator may come back after working very hard on the case and tell you he or she cannot help.

10. Discuss fees. The investigator should give you a clear, written list of all the fees involved in the search of your loved ones. There should be no hidden cost. If you decide to hire the investigator he or she should be able to give you a detailed account of every moment he or she has spent on the case. Ask for accounting of how you money is being spent. If an investigator "hedges" do not give him or her anymore money. You are paying for his time and you have a right to the accounting of it.

11. Ask the investigator what he or she can do that the police haven't done already. Sometimes, just having another person working on the case is enough, but if they are simply going to repeat everything that has already been done, you have to ask what the benefit of this will be. You should know exactly what you will be paying for.

12. A good investigator is willing to hand over all their findings to you and the police. Remember, a good investigator is working for you and with the police. You, as the family member of the missing loved one, are in control, not the investigator. If you feel the investigator is being too pushy or secretive, sever the relationship.

13. Report any unscrupulous investigators to the state. This way, no other family will fall victim to this scam.

Appendix Two

Hiring a Psychic

A discussion of tools for locating the missing would not be complete without a word about psychics. A psychic is a person who claims he or she can receive messages from an unknown source. There are many types of psychics. Some use tools, such as pendulums and tarot cards. Each psychic has his or her very own way of getting information. Though I believe in psychic ability and have worked with psychics my entire life, family members of the loved ones should be very wary when using a psychic, if they choose to use one at all. This is not a decision that should be made quickly, rashly or impulsively. It is not a decision that should be made out of desperation or frustration. Using a psychic, like any other decision made during the investigation, should be made after careful research and consideration.

The first thing anyone needs to know about psychics, even good ones, is they are human beings and the information they give you is not perfect. Psychics cannot perform miracles and no one should use a psychic and expect one. It is sad to report that psychics have done much more harm than good in the field of investigations.

The Do's and Don'ts of Choosing a Psychic

DO NOT use a psychic if he or she calls you "out of the blue." This is a sure sign that the psychic is feeling you out, seeing if they can get money from you. If a psychic contacts you out of the blue with a message, refer them to the police working on your case.

DO NOT use a psychic who asks for money; disregard him or her immediately, no matter how pressing or how much information the psychic seems to possess. This is a scam. I have not met one reputable psychic that will not work for free for families of the missing.

DO NOT use a psychic who refuses to work directly with the police. A good psychic will not only work with the police, but many police forces now know how to handle psychics. The police can match information the psychic gives them with what is already known and decide on what should be followed up on and what can be disregarded.

DO NOT expect miracles and do not trust a psychic who promises you one or "guarantees" anything. A psychic cannot guarantee anything.

DO NOT let a psychic interfere with the investigation. Always put your time and effort into the police investigation primarily. Any psychic information should supplement the police investigation, not replace it.

DO NOT choose a psychic based solely on a glitzy website. One of the best psychics I know does not have a website at all and only works by referrals and word-of-mouth. Anyone can create a website complete with testimonials.

DO NOT hang your hope on what the psychic says. Just like other information in your case it is only a small part of a whole.

DO get references. Good psychics can refer you to people they have worked for. Contact the references.

DO a web search of the psychic name. While all psychics have critics, be concerned about ones who are repeatedly reported as scammers.

DO go with an open mind. Allow yourself to disregard anything that doesn't sound right

DO get a recording of any session you do with the psychic or save any e-mails. If a psychic will not record his/her sessions, do not use him/her.

Again, I cannot caution you enough when using psychics. While reputable psychics are good and sincere people, the information they give you is from "unknown" sources and, as such, unverifiable. Proceed with extreme caution.

Works Consulted

Crater, Stella. *The Empty Robe*. New York, New York: Dell Publishing, Co., 1961.

Larsen, Anita. *Lost and Never Found II*. Scholastic, 1991

Maihafter, Harry J. *Oblivion: The Mystery of the West Point Cadet Richard Cox*. Brassey's Inc., 1999.

Tofel, Richard. *Vanishing Point*. Chicago, Illinois: Ivan R. Dee Publisher, 2004.

www.newspaperarchive.com

Acknowledgments

~ Todd Matthews, Doe Network, and NamUS, the guardian angels of the missing.

~ Dorothy Holmes Brown, whose brother Freddie is still missing

~ Susan Alfinito, whose brother Michael is still missing

~ Barbara Reeley, whose grandson Jaliek is still missing

~ Doug and Mary Lyall, whose daughter Suzanne is still missing

~ Kalli J. Lee, an advocate for the still-missing Kellisue Ackernecht

~ Kristen Freeborn, forensic artist

~ Jamie Richardson, private investigator

~ Stacy Jones, private investigator

~ Ripley, who works tirelessly for just a ball

~ Rita Argiros, who works with angels that just happen to take the form of dogs

~ Orange County Community College, for the generous use of their library

~ Cheryl Rice, whose friendship and editing skills were most appreciated

~ Vince Sanborn, whose great-great grandmother is still missing

~ John Joseph, whose niece Petra Muhammad is still missing

~ The Turks, whose daughter Audrey Herron is still missing

~ Daniel and Barbara Sullivan, whose son Brian is still missing

~ Sandra Poole, whose daughter Sharon Shechter is still missing

~ Amy Kusaywa, whose mother Judith Guerin is still missing

~ Eric Lake, whose father John is still missing

~ Keith Bran, whose witty banter sustained me throughout researching and writing this book

~ Finally, to all the missing and unidentified, not just in the State of New York but *everywhere…* we are working hard to bring you home